T0152423

TAKE THE FIRST SHOT

Praise for TAKE THE FIRST SHOT

"Peggy is a wise leader. She's a great career and personal development coach who has spent years studying human personality. You'll begin acting on it, and that's when your life will truly be revolutionized."

— Bob Proctor, international best-selling author and star of *The Secret*

"Peggy Caruso offers a treasure trove of small, practical, first steps you can take to revolutionize your life. Take one of her strategies and start creating a new future today!"

— Jack Canfield, Coauthor of *The Success Principles*
and *Chicken Soup for the Soul*

"Peggy Caruso shows anyone how they can use the biggest problems they face to their advantage and truly transform their life. One small step is all it takes and she gives you many possible ways to take that first step."

— Steve Harrison, Co-founder of The National Publicity Summit

"What makes Peggy's latest book so special is that it relates to every one of us and provides insight and ideas to make life easier! We all have seasons in life that are difficult and this book provides real help and real hope. Great read!"

— Linda K. Weis, State Farm Insurance Agent

"I have known Peggy Caruso and utilized her service at Life Coaching and Beyond, LLC, for almost three years for myself professionally, for my children and even my marriage. Peggy brings a very positive, professional and caring style. She is a problem solver and helps you become one as well. Peggy is a big believer in helping her clients to focus and to develop and follow a plan. She has a very goal-oriented approach and gives tools to help you succeed. Working with her has greatly benefited me and my family. I would recommend, and have recommended, her to others in need of her caring and professional services."

—Dave Trudell, System Director of Marketing and Communications

"When people ask Peggy to step into their lives they find themselves finding that last piece of the puzzle they were looking for. Peggy Caruso is the genuine definition of a professional coach. Everything from her unique style that devotes 100% of her energy to client success, to her application of advanced knowledge in her coaching practice — Peggy is serving the ever growing needs of her clients. I'm excited to see what Peggy is going to do next and how she will continue to have a positive impact on everyone's life with this book!"

— Joseph M. Fetzer, MBA, PC, Personal, Executive, and Business Coach

"Peggy's newest book has valuable content and has inspired me to take a shot at making some positive changes in my hectic life. From identifying my saboteurs to adding personal balance, I have become a more positive and happier person. Peggy's strategies as a coach are easy to implement and are quite effective. This book brings awareness to topics that I was overlooking during the hustle and bustle of my over-scheduled life. I am grateful to have found so many tips to reduce stress and reconnect with myself and enjoy healthier relationships!"

—Valerie Armanini

"Peggy's book has helped me to understand that finding the balance in your life is the key to personal happiness. If you have lost your footing and are looking for some easy, yet effective tools to create a better balanced life, this book is full of great information. This is definitely a must read for anyone interested in enhancing their life!"

— Judy Parolari

"Although I had long been aware of the value of self-reflection and had identified most of my faults, I never really understood the impact that my behaviors had on those around me. As my coach, Peggy not only helped me gain that understanding, she also coached me along a path of positive change in my leadership role, as well as in my personal life. She has since done the same for a long-time colleague of mine. I keep a copy of *Revolutionize Your Corporate Life* in my desk and use it to reinforce the things that Peggy has taught me."

— Kip Jones, Manager, Domtar Corporation

"As a life coach who is steadfastly dedicated to seeing her clients succeed, Peggy balances the right amount of personal encouragement and skill-building to help her clients manage their emotions, reframe their thoughts, and learn how to let go of things that are beyond their control. The life skills that she teaches — meditation, mindfulness, the law of attraction, non-reactivity, interpersonal relations — are skills that every functional adult needs to learn. My relationships and overall outlook on life have improved greatly thanks to my time working with Peggy, and I'm so thankful to have gained a new skill set to carry with me throughout all areas of my life."

—Lauren Johnson, Co-Founder, *Music & Mojitos*,
www.girlingothamcity.com

"Peggy Caruso, owner of Life Coaching and Beyond, LLC is a phenomenal coach. She is gifted with a unique understanding of what coaching is all about. She is very passionate about coaching and easily connects with her clients. Peggy is filled with a unique set of tools that allows her to get to the root of beliefs. Coaching with Peggy has changed my life. She has given me building blocks to assist me in recognizing how to build a foundation for the change. It is such a gift to be content, happy and positive. Peggy, you are truly a leader with an awesome, fantastic, ability for personal and professional life coaching."

— Linda Erich Mohr

"Peggy Caruso is a true blessing and my family feels very fortunate to have her as a life coach, trusted confidant, and especially as a dear friend. She is easily approachable and her warm and caring nature is endearing and welcoming to her clients. Peggy brilliantly inspires and empowers individuals with unique, simple, and effective coaching techniques that enrich their lives. While creatively encouraging accountability, she incorporates inspirational and positive affirmations to help you to be your best! Peggy is highly effective and talented in assisting parents, young adults, teens, and children overcome trials and tribulations with everyday life. I am especially grateful to her for giving my children the gift of lifelong empowerment. They found a new sense of balance, confidence, happiness, wisdom, motivation, and especially positivity. These qualities even extend beyond themselves and into the relationships of those surrounding them. Peggy's gift for life coaching will rejuvenate a passion within you to believe in yourself and discover your abilities, strengths, talents, and goals to achieve personal success!"

— Karen D. Miller

"I had the pleasure of meeting Peggy Caruso several years ago through her coaching business. Over the years she has coached me and my kids through many challenges in our lives. She has also become a dear friend and confidant. Her constant support and positive influence have been invaluable to me and my family. To quote my son at age 15, after he had his first coaching session with Peggy, 'Mom, everyone should have someone like Peggy to talk to.' I'm so grateful to have Peggy in my life."

— Jean Beckes

"I have known Peggy now for several years and I have personally witnessed her changing the lives of countless individuals. She has a unique approach to how she coaches. This is now her fourth book in the Revolutionize series. Peggy has been using her cornucopia of skills to make a difference in other people's lives. This book is a mere testament of the kinds of strategies she presents during her coaching sessions. Some might even call her a seasoned coach because [not only] does she incorporate her intellect and know-how, but she includes wisdom; wisdom and character that can only be developed through a lifetime. Peggy's methodology married with her life experiences has always been a recipe for success, not only for herself however, but for her clients as well."

— Neil A. Hanes

"About 4 years ago, I encountered one of the most influential persons in my life, Peggy Caruso. Peggy was referred to me when I was seeking help for my teenage daughter. Her life coaching not only helped my daughter, but me as well. We learned to build confidence within ourselves and to think more positively. She provided us the tools we needed to face any challenge we may encounter. During this time, I was contemplating divorcing my husband of 20 years. The relationship was toxic among other things and I lacked the confidence needed to make the decision that was necessary. I looked at things very negatively and often thought I wouldn't be able to do life on my own. Thanks to the life coaching provided to me by Peggy, I know otherwise. I am a single mother who supports her two children on her own and am acquiring my bachelor's degree online while working full time. My future is bright and I am loving it!"

— Ronnie Frey

TAKE THE FIRST SHOT

Strategies to Fire You Up and Change Your Life

— PART OF THE REVOLUTIONIZE® SERIES —

PEGGY CARUSO

NEW YORK

LONDON • NASHVILLE • MELBOURNE • VANCOUVER

TAKE THE FIRST SHOT

Strategies to Fire You Up and Change Your Life

© 2021 Peggy Caruso

All rights reserved. No portion of this book may be reproduced, stored in a retrieval system, or transmitted in any form or by any means—electronic, mechanical, photocopy, recording, scanning, or other—except for brief quotations in critical reviews or articles, without the prior written permission of the publisher.

Published in New York, New York, by Morgan James Publishing. Morgan James is a trademark of Morgan James, LLC. www.MorganJamesPublishing.com

ISBN 9781631951398 paperback
ISBN 9781631951404 eBook
Library of Congress Control Number: 2020936627

Cover and Interior Design by:
Constellation Book Services

Morgan James is a proud partner of Habitat for Humanity Peninsula and Greater Williamsburg. Partners in building since 2006.

Get involved today! Visit
MorganJamesPublishing.com/giving-back

DEDICATION

I feel the dedication is a very important part of a book. In my writing, I choose someone who inspires me throughout the process. I would like to dedicate this book to my daughter, Nikki. She is an exceptional person who has applied many of the techniques in this book and continually strives to excel in all areas of her life. Her parenting skills are exceptional, and it brings pride to my heart when I watch my grandson, Jordan, evolve into an exceptional young man. She and her husband, Chris, are deeply involved in Jordan's life and continually teach him great values. He has a strong inner core, and they should both be very proud.

The correlation between the techniques in this book and Nikki's life go hand-in-hand, both personally and professionally. She ties both areas together by working through her plan. She represents the importance of marriage and continually strives to enhance her relationship. Applying techniques in all of her relationships has shown the benefit of taking one shot at a time for building strong interpersonal relations.

Nikki has found the balance needed to parent her son. She allows him to advance with technology, but continually demonstrates the importance of incorporating sports and outdoor activities. She works on assisting him with the coping mechanisms needed to deal with other children who can be verbally cruel. It is human nature to have the desire to defend those we love; however, she incorporates mind-strengthening techniques to assist with handling obstacles.

Nikki continually amazes me with her talent and willingness to reach success. She has a wonderful gift with children. Also, receiving her certification as a life coach has allowed her to effectively coach children and teens. Everyone connects with her immediately. She was an amazing child who was a great influence on her brother. The bond they continually share is incredible. As a child, Nikki could find pleasure in the smallest of things and always had appreciation for everything; therefore, incorporating gratitude comes easily. I've watched her evolve into a wonderful adult, mother, sister, daughter, and friend. I stare at each chapter in this book and am filled with pride when I think of all of her positive attributes in relation to each area.

I talk briefly about the difficulties throughout our lives, and it amazes me how she remained a pillar of strength and love throughout. She has also been faced with elderly issues and death and has utilized techniques to ease the process. Throughout my life I've worked on becoming a great person and overcoming obstacles, but when I look at Nikki, I see someone who accomplished that talent throughout her childhood. She has always known the importance of forgiveness and never judges others. All of her qualities are areas most people work toward throughout life, but Nikki has been blessed with them from birth. I love you, and you will always be my little girl. I am so proud of who you have become. Wishing you a lifetime of love, health, happiness, and success!!!

Mom

ACKNOWLEDGMENTS

This book contains not only helpful information to the reader, but my life's passion to help others overcome obstacles. I love providing useful information to people on a personal and professional level. Many people have inspired me throughout my career and the process of writing this book.

Boundless thanks to Bob Proctor, international best-selling author, who changed my life in many ways. He provided the audio foreword for my "Revolutionize" book series and program. When I met Bob I was seeking positive change, and his teachings changed everything about me. I am forever grateful.

Throughout this process, Steve Harrison, co-founder of National Publicity Summit, has made a powerful impact on assisting me with my message and my mission. Thank you for the time you have given me and for the wonderful endorsement of my book.

There have been many influential teachers throughout my career (Dr. Steve G. Jones, Dr. Robert Anthony, Jack Canfield, and Wayne Dyer), whose teachings have allowed me to become a very successful executive and personal development coach, and author. Combining education with my life experiences has provided me the tools to assist others with overcoming adversities by incorporating a strategic plan of action.

Apart from education, numerous people in my personal life have inspired me, including my wonderful husband, Bob, who has been my sounding board and continues to support me on my journey. We have helped each other to overcome obstacles and continue to apply the techniques in this book to enhance our relationship. He makes it very easy to have a strong and healthy marriage. He is an inspiration throughout my endeavors, and his love, support, and help is everything I need. My friend, my love...my life.

My son, Joshua, is someone whom I love with all of my heart. He has endured many obstacles in his life, including a life-threatening illness that was debilitating at times. Our life wasn't always easy, and he was the "man of the house" even as a small child. His love and support are unconditional, and he has grown into a very fine man. I look at him and see a true person with a big heart. He has shown generosity from a young age and shares in my determination to succeed. He did very well in his educational process and has a true love of sports. Josh understands life and adversity and has the ability to make good choices both personally and professionally. He is wise beyond his years. I love you, Josh, and I am so very proud of you in every way.

Thank you for giving me a wonderful daughter-in-law, Kelly, who I am also very proud of. The two of you are going to be wonderful parents. It brings joy to my heart to see how you both work together to create a strong relationship that can overcome hard times. Kelly possesses the ability to balance life and has a kind heart. I am grateful.

My grandson, Jordan, also holds a spot near and dear to my heart. He also endures very serious health issues but remains positive and strong. He is a very well-rounded child with a heart of gold. He actually won a contest through Edgar Snyder & Associates, for his artwork about kindness. Edgar Snyder had a billboard placed with his picture and the artwork in his hometown. Jordan cares about people's feelings and is a genuine child. He loves the outdoors, scouting, and sports. His values come natural and continually mold him into a well-rounded young man. I love you, Jordan—always and forever.

To my wonderful son-in-law, Chris, who is also an outstanding parent and husband. I am forever grateful that we are family. You give so much of yourself and expect nothing in return. You are an amazing influence on Jordan and all those around you. I am blessed.

To the best mom and my best friend, Mary Ellen, for supporting me in everything I do. Her love is unconditional, and she is a true inspiration. I am grateful to all the wonderful memories we have. Your kindness and gentle nature prove that positivity and gratitude have a very strong impact on others.

I am also blessed with two special stepchildren, Lindsey and Kira, who are as close to my heart as my very own. Stepparenting can be a challenge, but the two girls have made it so easy because they have put much effort into building a strong family bond. Stepparents and stepchildren are just words. It doesn't make them any different from your birth children. I am grateful for the great relationships we have.

I am blessed with so many wonderful, supportive friends who are continually an inspiration, but a special thank you to Val and Dee, for helping me every step of the way with this book. You are amazing friends who are always there in good times and bad. That is true friendship. Thank you.

And to all of my clients who walked into my office for coaching and have left an imprint of friendship on my heart. I love you all.

I would like to thank Morgan James for their continued

support with my books. A special thank you to David Hancock, Jim Howard, Stephanie McLawhorn and all the staff that have worked toward making my book a success.

I am blessed.

Contents

I'll See You On the Other Side!

Close your eyes.... What if your life ended at this very moment?

Would you be able to say that you made a difference?

Thinking about the end of your life is dramatic so let's imagine more common situations when things go wrong.

Do you exhaust every effort to figure out what you did wrong and then implement a plan to turn it around?

How do situations go from happy to sad...profitable to destitute...health to sickness...trust to skepticism? In a world where changes occur so rapidly, we need tools and techniques that can assist us with turning those negatives to positives.

Over the past decade I've helped innumerable people overcome personal and professional obstacles. Being an expert problem solver allows me to assist anyone with identifying and changing negative behavioral patterns and put a strategic plan of action in place.

Finding the solution to alter our present state of mind when it endures confusion will help us set and reach goals.

It will create the mindfulness we need to improve our health and allow us to be successful and happy.

What does it mean to **TAKE THE FIRST SHOT**?

It is part of the books I write in the REVOLUTIONIZE series. It means to change or transform something radically or fundamentally by taking a step. In other words, it's time to ask yourself, "Are you ready for a new strategy?" This book is about strategies to fire you up and change your life!!

I am an executive and personal development coach, an eight-time entrepreneur and author, so it sounds like success was easy. Well, it wasn't. I raised two children, financially and emotionally, with no child support. There was a time when my children were very young, we lived in an apartment, and I was only making minimum wage. I was in several abusive relationships, lost my life savings, and had people steal from me. My son had a life-threatening illness, my sister took her life, and when my father died it separated me from my family. That was a difficult life. However, I chose positive changes, hard work, dedication, and the willpower to utilize every tool I offer in this book to turn my life around. Success was not easy for me, but looking back, I would never change any adversity. It made me who I am. I am strong, successful, and grateful, and I continually work on myself every day. I am far from perfect, but I love helping others and my mission is to make a difference in this world.

This book will help you by providing tools and techniques for overcoming obstacles in your own life. TAKE THE FIRST SHOT is often applied to basketball. Sometimes you begin with a small step to get into position to shoot a basket. Once you are in position, you take that shot with the faith and skill to make it. That is your strategy for a successful outcome. After you watch the ball go through the basket, you become motivated to play the game more aggressively. This makes you mentally stronger to attempt a 3-pointer. Think of the motivation from hearing the crowd: "Shoot it!! Take the shot!!"

WOW!!! Think about the power of the first shot you take. And better yet, think about the final shot that wins the game. Life is no different. We have many first shots to put us on the path to positivity, success, and happiness. Whether it's basketball or life, it's that first shot that takes a minute or less. We all know it is impossible to completely alter behavior or circumstances in a minute. It's the decision!!! The decision to begin taking action.

There are techniques that can provide a powerful start to resolving conflict within 60 seconds. Understanding the power of the first step will assist you on a pathway toward your goals. Taking a shot will motivate and help you understand that you can utilize that minute to either neutralize a situation or simply begin your journey toward a solution.

There is so much more to the game and to life than the first shot. Think of the entire game and how it relates to ongoing obstacles in your everyday life. You must continually fire multiple shots in different areas in order to maintain balance, both personally and professionally.

And also, think about the power of taking the final shot to win the game. Compare it to your life; taking the winning shot is equivalent to reaching your final goal.

This book is intended to guide you toward an understanding of behavioral patterns and the impact they have on your everyday life. Once you can recognize these patterns, then you'll learn what tools will assist in decision making, positivity, calmness, focus, and, most importantly, a resolution to rid yourself of negativity.

In order to put a strategic plan in place you must first be able to identify the saboteurs. One simple shot will provide you with the motivation to divide your plan down into manageable pieces and reach your desired outcome. So many of us realize we need to change many situations; however, it becomes difficult to understand where to begin. Taking a first shot will not provide you with the solution, but it will give you hope that ANY CHANGE IS BETTER THAN NO CHANGE.

Our personal and professional lives go hand-in-hand. We tend to lack balance between them. Whether you're aware of it or not, you bring your professional issues home and your personal ones to work. Take the first step to realize what needs to be changed and then take the shot to begin new and healthy habits. Sometimes, we fail to recognize there are any problems, so begin by slowing down. The shots will not provide you with a full plan for a solution, but they will move you toward a direction for positive growth.

The first chapter, **The Ebb and Flow of Your Relationships,** will provide you with insight into how relationships endure obstacles and the detriment to losing sight of the small things we tend to take for granted. Every relationship will have good times and bad; therefore, you need to be able to identify negatives so you can employ preventative measures for a happy and healthy relationship.

Chapter 1 will help you identify potential problems, and provide a shot for you to take, so you can begin to rectify the situation. You will then be able to utilize many shots to keep your relationship alive. Remember...the small things turn into big things. I can help you find the balance you need in this ever-changing circle of life.

The second chapter, **Connect the Dots—You Are the Connection**, will help you identify issues with your children and discover how your own behavior is affecting theirs. No one has the answers on how to be a perfect parent, but there are many shots you can take to eliminate negativity that affects the development of your child. You will learn how to recognize potential problems and redirect behavior for a successful outcome.

Children face challenges with communication, friendships, money, sharing, health, education, and the rapid growth of technology. It is our responsibility, as parents, to provide them with the proper tools that will help them make sound decisions as they grow and face challenges that lie ahead of them.

The third chapter, **Don't Just Make a Living...Make a Life**, about learning the significance of balancing career and family obligations, will assist you with time and stress management. All relationships endure ups and downs, but mixing a career into those relationships creates additional obstacles. Providing shots you can take creates a level of awareness that will help you identify and redirect certain behavior.

Your home life affects your career, and your career affects your home life. Learning how to set boundaries will help your family set and reach goals. Life itself can be very difficult, so learning how to balance the two will help you maintain a healthy lifestyle.

Think about the importance of finance and how it affects your entire family. But it's not just about making a living... it's about making a life. This is your life.

Chapter 4, **Invest in Yourself—Become a Better Person**, will help you with your own personal development. If you don't take care of yourself, your family and career will be affected. Self-improvement is something everyone should continually work on.

This chapter will offer tools to teach you self-reflection and awareness. Once you become in tune with your inner self, you will be able to enhance your clarity. You will be able to take shots that will help alter your behavior and have an impact on your personal and professional relationships.

Whether it's your relationships...your career...your environment...your health—it's about YOU! You can make the difference.

The fifth chapter, **Open Your Heart to Perfect Health**, is probably the most important chapter because if you don't protect your health, everything else will be affected. Health isn't just diet and exercise. It is also mindfulness, spirituality, and how you interact with those around you. Stress is in our everyday lives, but learning to control it is key. Even if you are physically fit, stress can cause major complications. I have personally experienced medical complications caused by trauma and stress. This chapter discusses indicators that will prompt you to take action to eliminate the stress.

Look into your heart and recognize the importance of your health.

Chapter 6, **Remember When? As Our Loved Ones Age**, will help you become aware of the importance of patience with the elderly. Taking care of our elderly loved ones can cause frustration. There are many shots you can take to help provide a sense of calmness so you can be more patient.

Imagine the confusion in their minds and the sadness in their hearts. Getting old is not only frustrating for the care-taker…it's frustrating for the patient. It is equally difficult to deal with physical health issues or conditions affecting the mind. Sometimes, the patient is suffering from both issues.

Learning techniques to help you calm down will allow you to regain your focus so you can provide the love, care, and support these people need. You may also be frustrated by the financial obligations of caregiving and the lack of support from other family members.

Learning how to transition into this difficult situation will allow you to CHERISH EVERY MOMENT.

The seventh chapter, **The Interpersonal Bond of Friend-ship**, explores the hardships of new and old friendships. It is extremely sad when a friendship endures animosity, so it's important you learn how to take shots to identify poten-tial problems and begin the process for repair.

There are also those friendships that experience so many complications that it is healthier to end them. Friendships don't necessarily have to be close relationships. They can be neighbors or acquaintances, so why not learn how to take a shot to display kindness?

This chapter will help you improve yourself, by first identifying any negative role you may play. You must be-come the friend you are looking for.

Chapter 8, **Love, Gratitude, Strength…Life**, is a combi-nation of four short stories about life.

We have one life to live and we are facing many complex situations. I have compiled a variety of solutions so you can begin to take a step toward positive change. Any step is better than no step.

Get started by getting ahead of the game....

Get ready for your new strategies!!!

Whether you realize it or not, you have just taken your own first shot by opening this book and beginning to read it....

By the time you complete this book you will have learned:

- How to identify potential problems
- To discover where negative behavior originates
- How to take a shot to begin the process toward making change
- The importance of taking multiple shots in every area

YOU ARE ON FIRE!!!

So, fire away at positive change and...

I'LL SEE YOU ON THE OTHER SIDE!!!

CHAPTER 1

The Ebb and Flow of Your Relationships

"Sometimes two people have to fall apart to realize how much they need to fall back together."
—Anonymous

"A successful marriage requires falling in love many times, always with the same person."
—Mignon McLaughlin

Relationships come and go like tides. You have fun... jump, swim, and laugh together in the waves of bliss. But, beware! There are rip currents that can pull you out, cause you to become temporarily disoriented, and put you in danger. When that happens, you need to swim harder and faster to get back to shore...your comfort zone. Beware of the undertows, which can drag you down and pull you under. Relax...it is temporary...BREATHE...you will pop back up. Once you land on shore there is a sense of calmness and you can regroup. Like a sand crab, you learn to keep your balance in the ever-moving sand of life.

I've helped many clients who have a range of relationship issues. You may be experiencing minor issues related to communication, romance, moods, habits, or work and family balance that can be resolved easily. Other, more complicated issues require more time and work to resolve. Whether you're facing a minor or major issue, taking one shot is better than doing nothing at all. One step moves you into action. That action step will move you closer to a strategic plan of action toward resolution.

COMMUNICATION

Kiss Your Frog. . .Turn Him Into A Handsome Prince!!

Women, you don't have to kiss a lot of frogs to find your prince. He is already your prince. Sometimes we just need to sprinkle a little fairy dust. Often, over time, your relationship may become boring or just routine.

For example, women say that their significant other would make positive gestures such as opening the car door, writing notes, buying flowers, and giving many compliments. What happens a year or two later? He still does everything except buying flowers. She is okay with it because he still does the other things. A year later he eliminates another gesture, and she is still okay because of the remaining two acts of kindness. However, what happens when he stops doing all of them?

She begins to focus on the fact that he doesn't do any of the things he did in the beginning of the relationship; therefore, she is sad. When this sadness increases, the relationship may begin to feel frayed. The same holds true for the woman who stops doing complimentary acts toward her significant other.

Many people feel as though keeping a relationship alive and healthy is difficult. However, it is not. It takes a minute or less per day to keep your relationship fun, positive, and loving. So...why don't we do it? We tend to get off track because we're preoccupied with daily family and work obligations. The day-to-day responsibilities can certainly take over.

Men, that may be the key to **MAKE THE GLASS SLIPPER FIT!** Your wife already has the glass slipper. Maybe it is just temporarily misplaced. It's lost in the chaos of family and work balance. I have worked with many people who say their partner doesn't notice the other individual. They seem to "lose that spark." Think of the previous story. Once you begin to see the decline in the positives, you need to bring it to your partner's attention. The number one issue is effective communication. So many people have lost the ability to communicate, or communicate effectively. When we are sad, we tend to become withdrawn. When we are angry, we tend to argue or fight. When we are content, we tend to be silent. And when we are happy, we tend to be busy with events, family fun times, or having our own "me time."

The other issue is fatigue. We get so busy taking children to their activities, with home obligations, with work, etc., that we become disinterested in one another at the end of the day. That's why we need to continually work on keeping relationships alive with minimal effort.

ROMANCE

How do we keep the romance alive?

Women: **CHANGE YOUR LIPSTICK!**

Take your shot to remind your partner how beautiful you are. Sound silly? Many men who have gone through my coaching program have indicated that their wives don't seem to put forth the effort of looking "extra nice" compared to the beginning of their relationship. I personally know many women (though not all of them) who admit that they can't wait to "get comfy" as soon as they get home. That's totally justified. These suggestions are just some helpful, easy tips to try. It is a shot toward change.

Take a shot by doing something. Changing lipstick is only one small suggestion. It's not about the lipstick; it is recognizing that something needs to change. I had a client change her lipstick and it actually made her feel better. She said that her husband noticed the change and he liked it as well. A win-win for both!!

Do you feel there are issues between you and your spouse? Even if your relationship is doing well, keep all of these easy suggestions in the forefront of your mind in case you ever feel as though you need a little boost to keep the spark alive. Think of all the "little" things you can do to make a "notice me" change.

As for you men...**CHANGE YOUR COLOGNE!** The cologne is your shot! Even if your partner doesn't notice, you can begin to communicate why you feel the need to make a change. There you have it—your second shot. Learning effective communication in your relationship will allow it to be a 3-pointer. Many people feel that they are good communicators, but effective communication is actually very complex because emotions tend to get in the way. Learning valuable ways to get your point across without pulling in negative emotion is something that should be included in your strategic plan of action. However, you can begin by letting your partner know that you recognize something needs to change.

Tiny physical changes make a difference. There are those who want to make bigger, physical changes and that's great, but don't get caught up in the thought process that change needs to be big. Any effort is great, so give it a try!

The other issue as to why your spouse has turned into a frog or has lost the slipper is because the person is making unflattering comments or behavior. Many people in relationships get so comfortable that they tend to blurt out comments when they are tired, frustrated, or simply having a bad day. Start to pay attention to what you say. Negative comments can turn into emotional abuse so **BEWARE AND BE AWARE!** Recognizing your own actions is the first step to repairing negativity. Once you become "aware" you will become heightened to "beware." That is the scary recognition about what can negatively happen. Heighten your awareness to your surroundings. How you communicate, or don't communicate, can make all the difference. Keeping romance alive requires a combination of physical changes, effective communication, and behavioral modification.

Maybe you just feel stuck or you need something different. **GET A NEW DO!** When we get a new hairstyle, we generally feel good. However, there are those times it doesn't turn out so well. Try to remember...it's just hair. It will grow. I myself felt as though I needed a change, so while on vacation I made an appointment at the hair salon in our hotel. Well...be careful what you ask for. Change is what happened. It was the worst haircut ever, but I laughed. I knew it would grow out and my husband was very supportive. I found different ways to style it so I wouldn't focus on how short it was. I actually had to place bobby pins in it every day for eight months so it didn't look like I had wings.

I've talked to many men and women who get a new hairstyle and their spouse hates it. So, what happens? Someone gets their feelings hurt. If your spouse tries something new, be supportive. Understand that it can be fixed or that it will grow out. Remember, I will continually remind you that every problem has a solution.

As a coach, I provide strategic plans of action to assist people with change, both personally and professionally. However, to implement those types of changes, you always need to begin slowly...take the first shot. In coaching we call it "breaking it down" into manageable pieces. The first shot is a small step to making change. The reason the first step or shot is the most important is because you are proving to yourself that you have the ability to begin setting a new goal with new behavioral patterns. Remember, if I hand you a big plan, it won't work until I get to know your strengths, weaknesses, habits, etc. As I have stressed, that first shot will motivate you, and any step toward improvement is amazing.

AWARENESS

The initial step in every situation is recognizing what needs to be changed. Once you take that step, you'll then have the ability to take a shot. That shot is action. Sometimes, you will take a shot and miss. Don't be discouraged if your spouse doesn't recognize the new lipstick or cologne. You may have to make a second attempt at your shot.

Think back to the beginning or when things were better. What's different? Many people have had difficult relationships while others haven't. However, it is easy for a relationship to experience difficulty without us realizing it. Try hard not to blame the other person. We tend to be able to recognize negative patterns in others, but the real improvement is when we recognize what we are doing wrong. We can ALL do things better. So, **OWN IT AND OUTLINE IT!** Owning what you do wrong is an amazing shot. It is taking 100% responsibility for your actions... past...present...and future!! The mistakes you have made in the past come from habits and fears and affect what you are still doing wrong in the present. Being in an abusive relationship tends to make you feel sorry for yourself. I know I used to feel like, "Why me? I'm a good person who doesn't deserve this." However, once I realized I needed to take ownership of my role, I was able to overcome the self-pity. I needed to understand and own the fact that I allowed the behavior. Once you allow abuse, in any manner, you become part of the problem.

Once you recognize behavior from past mistakes, you will be able to alter what you are presently doing wrong.

The recognition will provide you with insight to see how your actions will affect you going forward (future). Owning it will allow you to put preventative measures in place for positive growth. Taking ownership of negative behavior is a basic fundamental principle toward happiness and success. Why? Because you can't make positive changes without realizing what you are doing wrong and where the behavior comes from.

Once you begin to change it is easy to implement small acts of kindness. There are many small things that take minimal effort to let your spouse know that you love and appreciate him or her. **SHARPEN YOUR PENCIL!** When we begin our workweek after a nice weekend, we allow the responsibilities to override positivity and appreciation. Buy some sticky notes: you can write things like...

"I love you."
"Have a great day!"
"I appreciate you."
"We are going to have the best week...ever."

You can also write notes to say you are sorry. If you have difficulty discussing argumentative scenarios, it is sometimes easier to write your thoughts.

So, you see, there are many simple, short notes you can write. And since we all have cell phones, **CAPTURE THEIR HEART!** It only takes seconds to send a text message or emoji that will make your spouse feel great. You can also do things like that for your children. Place a sticky note in their backpack or on their bed. I used to write a note to my children and place it in their lunchbox. Then to really capture their heart, I would take a bite out of the middle of their sandwich. Just a small one ☺. It certainly made an impact because one day when my son was home from college, I made him a sandwich and he just stared at it. I asked him what was wrong, and he said, "I don't think I can eat it. It doesn't have a bite taken out." So, as you can see, quick, little notes (and little bites) make a huge difference. It's a shot to show you love them.

So often we get caught up in emotion, which becomes a part of our behavioral patterns. We tend to react if something isn't good enough. So, when disappointment sets in... **EAT THE BURNT TOAST!**

I read a nice story about a wife who made burnt toast for her spouse and child. After the husband ate the toast, he told her it was the best toast he ever had. When the wife walked away, the child asked the father why he told the mom he liked it when he knew it was burnt. The father said, "She went out of her way to make it for us." So... eat the burnt toast and appreciate the effort. A very high percentage of people would complain or throw it away. Try to think about the effectiveness of how that positive reaction will change her day. Also, think of the impact it would have on the child. Win-win for all!

LAUGHTER

Eating the burnt toast is your shot to appreciating who and what you have. If you don't appreciate the idiosyncrasies, then your thought process will grow exponentially in a negative manner. You wouldn't notice that you could take two immediate shots at making someone feel great. After you "eat the burnt toast" you can incorporate happiness with laughter. **LAUGH—IT'S THE BEST MEDICINE!**

> *"An optimist laughs to forget; a pessimist forgets to laugh."*
> —Tom Nansbury

There are so many shots you can take relative to laughter. To overcome small irritants, you can incorporate laughter. I am an OCD person, which is a difficult quality because I get out of my comfort zone when things aren't neat and organized. With OCD, you have an added level of stress, especially if you are surrounded by people who don't have it. Simple things like leaving a drawer open, forgetting to throw Keurig cups in the garbage, failing to push a chair in, clothes laying around, and basic clutter creates negativity for me.

I work on myself every day, so the first step was to realize those types of things are my issue (remember, I talked about recognizing). I would continually be upset with others if I didn't find a way to cope. So, I incorporated laughter. I display solutions to present a way to fix each one without turning it into anger and frustration. Instead of complaining I would say, "Watch." Then I would throw the Keurig cup in the garbage and make a silly sound. After a while, they would throw it away and make the same sound. Or, I would twirl around and push the drawers closed with my feet and hands. I know it sounds silly, but the way I displayed myself helped them realize it only takes seconds to complete the tasks. The silliness lightened the mood and avoided an argument. The end result: they laugh at the silly presentation, and it restores harmony. Everyone wins.

If your spouse has a bad day and negativity is presenting itself, there are many small things you can do to "take a shot" at diffusing the situation. Find something you can do together that will **LIGHTEN THE LOAD!** This is a shot to remove pressure of responsibility by helping your spouse. Understand what the other person is experiencing and watch for signs so you can recognize the irritant. Take over and take control. Think about the things that can overwhelm us. We become anxious if we have a lot of responsibilities and not enough time to accomplish those tasks. Remove some of the burden with daily obligations by helping with dishes, laundry, or outdoor chores. Be the better spouse.

Don't just stop there. After you have helped, your spouse will be relaxed and then you can **SHAKE YOUR BOOTY!** That may sound silly, but if you turn on music, grab your spouse, and begin dancing, it will automatically lighten the load on the person who is stressed. It's a way of saying, "I'm sorry you are stressed." Many of you will say that these steps don't interest you or are pointless. Then be creative based on your personality. There are so many things you can do to tie in man/woman responsibilities. **LIGHT THE FIRE!** Take a night and cook together. And it's not always about the man helping the woman. She can light his fire by going outdoors with him and building a fire where they can sit, talk, relax, and enjoy!!

MINDFULNESS

Remember, these are small suggestions and if they don't work for you, they may prompt you to **THINK OUTSIDE THE BOX!** See, that's a shot! Use your imagination and creativity. What are some things your spouse likes to do? What are some things you did together when you were dating? Think about what makes him or her laugh. It's not hard. We make it hard because we are caught up in the hustle and bustle. Slow down for what is really important—your relationship!! We have a spiral staircase in our home and there are times when I place rose pedals on the treads, write notes, and buy small gifts. It's a nice gesture to let my husband know that I love and appreciate him and it takes minimal effort.

Take a break from the daily responsibilities and RE-MEMBER the qualities of your partner that initially attracted you. Life is so very short. Please take time to put things into perspective.

Bob Proctor taught me about the six mental muscles, and I have researched the importance of them on my own. I've educated myself as to why they play such an important role in recognition and creating new habits.

These muscles are:

1. Memory
2. Reason
3. Perception
4. Imagination
5. Willpower
6. Intuition

I teach the importance of how our mental muscles impact our goals. As you begin to see positive results, you will automatically be working your mental muscles for good. Mental exercises are like physical ones. For example, when you do sit-ups, you get sore. Once you push forward the soreness goes away and you increase performance. Mental is the same; however, we can't see or feel it, so we tend not to recognize it. Once you understand them, you will be able to make the correlation in every situation. Let's take this entire chapter about relationships and do a comparison.

Once you begin the "recognition" process you will be able to utilize your memory. You will become aware of how things used to be and compare it to what has changed. Once you are aware, you will be able to reason by creating the formation of ideas to support your new habit. You will then be able to change your perception or point of view. Utilize your imagination with the creation of how you want it to be. I feel as though imagination is key in goal setting. Pull in your senses. (Sights? Sounds? Smells? Taste? Feel?) Your willpower is your motivation to make it happen, and intuition is your sixth sense that allows you to trust your internal feelings. It sounds easier than it is.

You need to begin with that first shot that will provide you with the motivation and dedication toward positive growth.

TEMPERAMENT

There are times we get grumpy from the daily stressors. It turns into self-sabotage, so...**TURN GRUMPY INTO HAPPY!** Grumpy, as one of the seven dwarfs, was negative, rude, condescending, and quite opinionated. Though stubborn, he was compassionate and refused to admit it. He was quite intelligent and fearless. So, you see, we all have a little of both, and although someone may seem to be "grumpy" all the time, find what makes them happy. Better yet, figure out what makes them grumpy. Once we discover the negative notion of causing the bad mood, we can then find a solution toward the positive. Sometimes, we all need a nudge to bring out the positive side (our own little soft spot). There are many circumstances that can affect us negatively.

Until you are able to help figure out what is making someone grumpy, be conscientious of the person's mood! **DON'T POKE THE BEAR!** This is where you pick and choose your battles. If you are around someone who has a bad temper, or if they are abusive, do not purposely aggravate the situation. If they are screaming at you or their temper has flared, don't say anything. Just try to diffuse the situation by attempting to turn the conversation positive.

There are always times where we can give in and allow the other person to win (even if you know you are right). What's the harm? However, please be cautious. Don't continually give in because you may set a new habit and become a doormat. If it is a serious situation, you must EFFECTIVELY communicate your point. I discuss effective communication a lot and that is because it is key in every situation.

You always begin a conversation (even if you are angry) with a compliment. Don't make it false. We all have something within us that is a good attribute. Focus on what your partner does do right instead of what the person does wrong. Example: Let's say you hate grocery shopping, so your spouse continually does it for you. When you are irritated, focus on what he/she does for you to alleviate your stress. If your partner has done something serious to upset you, of course you will discuss the problem. However, start with the positive. Ask questions so the person can have an "aha" moment to understand how he or she contributed to the problem. Stay calm and keep your voice monotone. That will allow you to connect to the calmness within the person. Once you have discussed a serious situation and find resolution, you must move on in a positive manner.

CREATIVITY

Once you realize the good your spouse does, then go the extra mile. **MAKE THEIR DAY!** This is taking a shot toward the element of surprise. It is not intended to have you "jump out" and scare your spouse. The intent is for you to come up with a surprise that is out of the ordinary. Remember, too, that surprises don't have to be expensive purchases. A surprise can be the simplest act of kindness to let someone know you recognize and care. Pay attention to something your spouse has been talking about. He or she will be thrilled to see that you remembered. If you are unsure of details, make them a card or coupon that states you're presenting the person with a specific surprise.

Everyone loves a surprise, and I always encourage writing a love note or letter. It allows you to become aware of all the things you love about your spouse. Speaking of letters...**CREATE A BOX!** This is a very unique idea. Purchase a decorative box; place a very nice piece of fabric inside; lay a bottle of wine and two glasses (or whatever you like); and then each of you write a letter and place it in a sealed envelope. Place all of those items inside and set it aside for a year (preferably do this on your anniversary). If you get into a bad argument and don't feel as though you're coming to a resolution, open the box, pour the wine, and read the letters. It will be a reminder of your love. If opening the box early becomes an option, hopefully you will feel badly for not reaching the yearly goal of happiness and celebration. Feeling badly is supposed to help you to find a resolution for the argument.

If you get past the argument, wait until the year is up and then open the wine and read the letters. Place a new bottle of wine and write two new letters and keep doing the same thing year after year. It is a wonderful idea that really helps. You feel very good when you don't open it until the year is up and you get to celebrate.

Try to keep in mind, relationships endure many challenges with child responsibilities, financial obligations, work/life balance, and time and stress management. **FIND THE BEAUTY IN THE BEAST!** Take a shot to find beauty in your relationship and within each other. We all have negatives and areas we can improve on. It is difficult to eliminate fears and bad habits and make behavioral changes, but recognizing what needs to change is the first step. Find the beauty in the area that brings you down. For example, while enduring abuse and negativity in my relationship, I continually focused on the positive aspects of the family members who brought me joy. You must still deal with the negativity, but for a moment you can redirect your thoughts to what makes you happy. Those moments will bring a sense of calmness so you can think clearly.

Whatever is bringing you down and causing negativity is the beast. You can always turn the negative situation to positive. In many cases, parents will share thoughts with me, about their children, when they are being disruptive. A brief example: If your beast is frustration with your child, find what makes him or her happy and focus on that. As parents, we tend to get angry about the negative behavior of the child. Begin to question why the child is angry or disruptive and then you will be able to begin turning the situation around. Or, if you are experiencing financial diffi-culties, find something that you can do together as a family that doesn't cost anything. To take a shot takes minimal effort. In one minute or less, you can take action that shows you that every plan begins with a shot!!!

I can't provide you with a magic wand, but I can offer tools that will help steer you in the right direction to overcome obstacles. **USE YOUR MAGIC!** Take a shot to use the magic of your mind. Your mind is a powerful tool that can place you on the path to personal development. It's like magic. We use a very small percentage of our mind; therefore, utilize the tools in this book that will assist you with strengthening your mind. Sometimes our wand gets bent. You can straighten it and make it strong. Relationships are at the core of all the other matters in life. Relationships are not just spouse issues. They involve friends, co-workers, strangers, healthcare providers, and so many others. We can make it complicated or we can make it simple...you decide.

Once you've made an investment to make your relationship the very best it can be by releasing the negative and replacing with the positive (EBB AND FLOW), you can now focus on your parenting skills.

CHAPTER 2

Connect the Dots—You Are the Connection

"The best kind of parent you can be is to lead by example."
—Drew Barrymore

"A person's a person, no matter how small."
—Dr. Seuss

STOP—LOOK—LISTEN

Think of all the areas of involvement with your children. You need to stay on top of their feelings, habits, fears, friendships, bullying, school issues, extracurricular activities, and communication. It's exhausting to think about all of it. We as parents are responsible for them financially, spiritually, emotionally, and their overall well-being. We oftentimes become so wrapped up in all those responsibilities that we become overwhelmed. Don't be hard on yourself when you miss the signs. Every parent can do some things better, but overall, I think most do the best they can to connect the dots. Remember...you are the connection that bridges the gap in all aspects of the child's life.

In my experience, I've seen every imaginable situation from mild to severe. This chapter is intended to assist you with slowing down and taking a shot to make situations better for you and your children. **STOP—LOOK—LISTEN!** is your shot to first discover if there are any addressable issues, and if so, what are they?

Close your eyes and think about these questions:

- Is your child happy or sad?
- Are they experiencing any negativity with school or friends?
- What are their innermost thoughts?
- Most importantly...do you know?

Once you stop and slow down, you will be able to assess your child's life. Listening is a tool we can all use. We get so busy in the doing that we miss even the simplest of things. Get to know your child all over. So, you see, it is actually three shots. If you get one right, you are ahead of it.

ROLE MODEL

Pay attention to what you are doing and what other parents are doing. Consider this powerful quote by Frederick Douglas:

"It is easier to build strong children than to repair broken men."

Think about these words. You have the opportunity to fix so many things when your children are young. The first shot you can take is to **FIND A NEW FRIEND!** So many parents spend so much time focusing on being their child's friend that they don't see the damage that it's causing. Children can figure their friendships out on their own. They are going to encounter great friends and mean ones as well. We, as parents, need to guide, educate, strengthen, and support them. Don't always come to their defense. Allow them to work through the tough times. It will make them stronger and wiser. If you make all the decisions for them and continually bail them out on every little thing that upsets them, how will they learn and grow?

If you continually treat them as a friend, you will create an entitled child. I have worked with many young teens and adults who admit they are entitled and want to change. Some of them can see the detriment, and then there are those clients who are entitled and will become worse as grown adults. Sometimes when we entitle children, they become overwhelmed by the pressure of the parents.

There are no set rules for raising children so we need to do as much information gathering to see what works and what doesn't. Assisting your child with focus, slowing down, and being responsible will allow them to have plenty of kid time. Let them be a kid and learn how to grow.

PARK THE BULLDOZER! I'm sure you've heard the phrase "bulldozer parent." Take a shot to park it. This type of parent wants to plow all obstacles from their lives and prevent their child from having to face adversities or failure. Failure is good. It is a steppingstone to success. Sure, it is difficult for any parent to see their child struggling or experiencing hurt, but it is far more beneficial for the child to learn from those setbacks. Parking the bulldozer is a big shot in the right direction.

I work with many children who have parents who do everything for them. This causes them to struggle with coping mechanisms, and it can also cause mood swings. Teaching them coping mechanisms will allow them to become emotionally stronger and prepare them for adulthood. If they become reliant on a parent doing every little thing and solving every little problem, how will they function as an adult?

AWARENESS

In order to assist you with discovering where your children are in life, you need to heighten your awareness. In coaching, we begin by discovering the self-awareness of the individual and their surroundings. Secondly, you assess the needs, values, and beliefs, which is their inner core. If your child encounters friends or circumstances that do not coincide with their inner core values, then you begin by asking empowering questions. Those questions will assist you in figuring out who or what is causing issues.

Sometimes when children show signs of negative change, parents tend to push them harder. There are instances where parents are overly driven to ensure perfection within the child and make them participate in too many activities. The overload becomes detrimental to the child's mental and physical well-being. **CALL A TIMEOUT!** Take the shot to call a timeout and redirect what you are doing. Keeping our children involved in activities is a great thing because it teaches them accountability and team-building exercises and helps keep them busy so they don't get in trouble. Call a timeout to assess the needs of your child and if he or she is too involved. This will help you create balance between school and home. There are children who can handle a lot, but there are so many instances where children internalize on the pressure. It can cause many negative issues within the child, and they can acquire new, unhealthy habits. It can also affect their study habits.

HOCUS, POCUS, GAIN YOUR FOCUS! All children need focus. Taking the shot to call a timeout will allow them to slow down, take a breath, and have the ability to focus more on schoolwork, while creating balance for home responsibilities. To get a child to focus you need to break down the child's routines into manageable steps. As I stated with too many activities, the same holds true for daily routines. It will assist with self-control and structure.

For example, parents introduce technology earlier and earlier, so be careful. Too much technology time affects focus and communication. Lack of focus and communication can lead to major complications. One of the major issues I see in child coaching is the issue of cutting. In my experience, children who cut do not know how to release emotions or have the ability to communicate what the negativity is. It is important to get your child to verbalize, rather than text. It's time to heighten your awareness with focus and look for signs relative to cutting. I am sure there are many other signs. Below are the ones associated with my experience as a coach.

SIGNS AND SYMPTOMS OF CUTTING

- Depression or anxiety
- Changes in relationships
- Lack of communication
- Mood swings
- School performance
- Bruises or cuts
- Wearing long-sleeve shirts

TECHNOLOGY

Technology needs to be monitored very carefully. **GET TO KNOW THE STRANGER—ELIMINATE THE DANGER!** This is a very important shot to take. I've dealt with many dangerous situations regarding children becoming involved with strangers. It usually begins very innocently. There are so many chat rooms or apps that look innocent, but when the child becomes actively involved, he or she can get drawn into dangerous situations. Below are a few, but be aware that new ones appear often.

- MeetMe is an app where teens can be in contact with users who are much older.

- Skout is a flirting app that's used to meet and chat with new people.

- TikTok is used for sharing user-created videos that contain bad language and adult content.

- Kik is specifically for kids, but anyone can join and contact or direct-message your child.

- LiveMe is a live streaming app, but you don't know who's watching and your child's location is revealed.

- Holla is all about connecting strangers from around the world through video chat.

- Whisper is a social confessional where children remain anonymous, but share their feelings. It can reveal your child's location.

- ASKfm encourages people to ask questions, which opens the door for online bullying.

There are many more, and as I stated, new ones emerge continually. I've seen parents who continually educate their child on stranger danger, but many parents are not technologically savvy. If you aren't educated on all aspects of your child's technology than hire someone to assist you. There are many informational tools on the internet for you to self-educate on issues like parental blocks.

Stranger danger is not the only issue linked with social media and chat rooms. I've worked with families to identify sites that are linked to pornography. I've seen how children accidentally stumble onto a bad site, and it has a very detrimental impact on them. I've also experienced a child who came in contact with a dangerous person from a different state. While working with the family and the police, we discovered that whoever is responsible for making contact first is liable. All states have different laws relative to these issues so your child could be liable relative to another state's law. We need to implement precautionary measures to ensure the safety of all children.

Technology can be used for good and children need to keep up with it; however, it is imperative that you know what your child is doing on the internet and who they are conversing with. Take away some of the tech time and replace it with productive time.

RESPONSIBILITY

Then...**SCORE THE CHORE!** Take a shot for responsibility. Every child should be assigned chores. It teaches them responsibility, while gaining a sense of appreciation for what it takes to run a household. Many parents will ask me my thoughts on allowances. I feel you should call it "contribution." It is okay to pay them for extra-ordinary chores, but there are those that should be a daily requirement. When they are young, begin with a scorecard where you keep track and give them points. Once they earn so many points, contribute a monetary reward. If finance is an issue, you can reward them in other ways. Create a "family fun day" or allow them to invite a friend over. Be creative!

Think about the increased self-esteem that will come from your children doing chores. It will help in multiple areas of their lives. For example, children who do chores regularly learn the value of being part of a team. It also provides them with a sense of accomplishment, and it will assist them with understanding the importance of having a routine. There are many sample chore charts on the internet. It is a win-win for all!!

LAUGHTER

Chores actually helps children with moods. Many children get angry with their parents when a chore is assigned, but if you begin the habit when they are very young it will become habitual. When you experience a bad mood in your child, you can make it lighthearted. Try to remember, adults experience mood swings as well.

BE A HUMOR MODEL! Children love to laugh. Research many of the Disney movies and all the life lessons they teach. They actually demonstrate the importance of coping mechanisms and highlight the benefits of laughter. My daughter was always laughing as a child. She is three years older than my son and they are so very different. She knew seventeen nursery rhymes by the time she was two, so when my son was that age, I noticed he didn't talk very much. I began to become concerned, so I talked to our family doctor. He laughed and said, "Your daughter does all the talking for him." I began to notice he was correct. Every time I would take them for a walk, there would be people who stopped to talk. When they would ask him his name she would answer. She was her own humor model.

There are times children are a little tired or grumpy, so it's always fun to try and turn it to humor. I can remember when my son was young. He woke up one morning and was a little grumpy. Of course, that makes morning more difficult when everyone is stressed to get out the door. I looked at him and said, "Did you know that if you go back in your bed and get out on the other side, you will be happy?" He went to his room and when he came out into the kitchen, he said, "Mom, did you know it works? I went back in and got out on the other side and now I am happy."

How simple was that? Will that technique work for everyone? Maybe not, but it is a way to show you that you can be creative and simply try. Many adults don't take the time to realize they wake up grumpy at times, so anytime you can lighten a mood, it will lighten your environment.

Moods affect how kids interact in school. Pay attention to become aware if there is a link to bullying issues.

BULLYING SYMPTOMS

- Change in sleep patterns
- Change in eating patterns
- Mood swings, including sadness or anger
- Continually complaining of being ill and not wanting to attend school
- Withdrawn
- Silent and wanting to spend time alone
- Lack of friends
- Insecure
- Behavioral issues
- Bruises or cuts
- Failing grades

If your child is being bullied, **ENCOURAGE...DON'T DISCOURAGE!** Teach them things like how to say "no" confidently or not show fear. If you, as a parent, have a reaction that is loud and abrasive it will make your child more nervous. Attempt to teach them how to cope and safeguard against the bully. Use it as model to help them gain strength and confidence. If the bullying is severe, you must seek outside assistance. A bully will continue to do so if the person knows that the child is affected by his or her bullying. Begin to take your shot by trying to determine the severity level. If it's minimal, encourage them by teaching positive coping mechanisms. If it is more severe, take a second shot by seeking assistance.

We have become very sensitive about bullying, but be careful what you classify as abuse. I have had many parents who will talk to me about their child being bullied and when they are finished describing the incident, it's not actually bullying. History proves that you will always have some children who say mean things to others. We need to teach our children coping mechanisms so they can defend themselves against name calling or minor issues. My favorite quote is by Eleanor Roosevelt:

"No one can make you feel inferior without your consent."

I had a severe case of bullying that I helped someone with. The child was on crutches and a group of children kicked the crutches out from under them and began to spit on the child. That is a case of bullying that needs to be reported. There was another case where someone drew a picture of a person shooting the child and blood dripping down their face. Those are situations that can mentally scar a child. In coaching we teach coping mechanisms, but in severe cases it requires an additional response to an outside intervention.

Go back to the first shot of stop—look—listen. You should see the signs if your child is being bullied. Also, look for signs to ensure your child isn't the one doing the bullying. It isn't always true, but many students who bully others have tendencies of being aggressive and insecure and having poor social skills. They also lack empathy toward others.

Just remember, parenting can be difficult. You will be ahead of the game if you **CHANGE YOUR BOO-HOO!** In the movie *Monsters, Inc.*, children were believed to be toxic in the beginning. The outcome was that the character Boo overcomes fears and proves not to be toxic. Initially, monsters got their energy from a child's scream, but in the end, they find that they get more energy from capturing their laughter. It is no different in real life. It is imperative we eliminate negativity in our children so they can become more productive as adults. We become much more positive, energetic, focused, and loving when we eliminate fear, overcome obstacles, and incorporate laughter. Take your shot and change your boo-hoo from screams and negativity to laughter and positivity.

There are so many things we need to teach our children to help them become successful adults. I did many things wrong as a parent and my parents did things wrong. Our children will make mistakes as well, but try to keep an open mind and heart. Pull in as many lighthearted shots that you can. Laughter is the best medicine. Take the small shots to make them well rounded, and if they don't work, take another shot.

FINANCE

I have mentioned chores and financial contributions, which is really the beginning of incorporating financial teachings. I've coached many children and I teach them success principles. It makes a huge difference. Children are actually really good with finance. They generally want to earn money and do good. I continually teach **SAVE—SPEND—SHARE!** It has such an impact. When I give them a monetary gift, I have a letter to accompany it explaining the importance of the three S's. Divide the money into three parts. The first one is for saving. Teaching them to save will show the reward of building a significant amount of money. The purpose of saving can be taught by showing the benefit of what they can do with a large amount of money later in life. You can also teach them the power of being able to spend a portion of it on something they have wanted for a long time. One thing I used to do with my children was to have them use a portion of their savings on something they wanted that was expensive. For example: When they wanted a trampoline, I didn't just purchase it for them. I put in a certain amount and made them contribute a percentage. When they have to give up a part of their savings, they tend to appreciate it more.

The second part is for spending. All children love to spend, but when you teach them that they can only spend a portion, they become more aware of what they truly want vs. what they can do without. Begin by letting them make small purchases and point out the cost of the item and the use of it. Explain the value of the product and then allow them to decide if they really want or need it.

The third is for sharing. It teaches them to be aware of those less fortunate, therefore creating a sense of gratitude for what they do have. Plus, giving creates the thought process of charitable organizations that help others in need. It gets them to continually think of how they can make a difference. I've always involved my children in the power of giving/sharing. When they were young, we were actively involved in the angel trees at Christmas. I made them give a portion of their savings to the gift. Think about how something so simple will impact them as they become an adult.

When I was in my 20s and financially struggling, I can remember going to the store and having to choose between being able to purchase toothpaste or deodorant. Even though it was a very difficult time I still set aside coins in my sharing jar. It kept things in perspective. I used it for mind strengthening by telling myself that someone out there is in a worse situation and that my present state was only temporary.

It is a great way to teach them responsibility with finance. Now is your chance...**CLOSE THE BANK!** Allow your children to learn how to give from their own earnings and stop giving them free access to your money. No thought will be given to something that they didn't earn. The expectation from you handing them money creates entitlement. Many parents give credit cards to their teenagers. That is very dangerous. I've personally coached children who were given a credit card and it made it very easy for them to purchase illegal items. Credit cards can be a very good way to teach your child about building credit, but save this strategy for when they attend college. Educate them on interest rates and how to avoid extra charges by paying the bill in full each month. Once they understand the amount of interest charged by the credit card companies, and how it impacts them, they will become more conscientious on spending. Make sure to teach them how it can affect their credit positively (pay it off immediately and build credit) or negatively (charging too much on the card and not paying on time).

Teaching children financial skills helps prepare them to be responsible adults and also alleviate their fears about money. When my daughter first received her driver's license, she had an accident. She reached to the floor to pick something up while driving and struck the guardrail. I remember her being very upset, but I used it as a teaching moment. I kept her in the loop as to the financial obligation of having to get the car fixed. She was very apprehensive about driving again, but I made her get back in the car. I was truly grateful no one was hurt, and I feel as though it helped her become a more conscientious driver.

Once you've taken your shots to CONNECT THE DOTS (bridging the gap between you and your children).

Now, take the time to discover ways to create the balance you need for your career and family obligations.

CHAPTER 3

DON'T JUST MAKE A LIVING. . . MAKE A LIFE

"What you get by achieving your goals is not as important as what you become by achieving your goals."
—Zig Ziglar

"Knowing others is intelligence
Knowing yourself is true wisdom.
Mastering others is strength.
Mastering yourself is true power."
—Lao Tzu

There are so many people I've worked with who experience difficulty with balancing career and family obligations. Your every action affects both areas of your life, and those actions can create time and stress issues. Stress can cause many obstacles in life and health. There are many people who stay so focused on the day-to-day routine and obligations that they miss very important signs. Signs that can affect career and family. This chapter is intended to assist you in discovering saboteurs and provide tools to help you begin change toward positive growth. A happier home, a positive working environment, and healthier relationships. Begin your balance.

S.O.S.—SEEK OUT SILENCE!

A powerful shot you need to take in all areas of your life!! Master this shot and you will be on fire!!!

Think about the continual chaos we all endure at home and at work. If we could devise a plan to begin fixing it, think about the importance of silence. Silence teaches us to learn great listening skills, while creating a sense of calm. One problematic area is our cell phones. It is an area most people don't want to discuss or work on. Why? Are we that connected?

I frequently discuss heightening your awareness. Well... start becoming aware of everyone around you and how so many of us are connected to electronics. I am a business-person who is very connected to my clients; therefore, I receive continual correspondence from them throughout my day. However, I have learned how beneficial it is to set boundaries for creating personal space. As long as you communicate with the people who need to know, you can disconnect.

If you have a career outside the home, think about the hours you're away from that environment. When you come together with those you love, you should be able to disconnect. And...you should convey that same message to your spouse and children. There is no reason anyone should have electronics at the dinner table or when involved with family obligations. Enjoy the moment...enjoy each other.

Likewise, when you get to work, silence your phone. If there is an emergency, your loved ones know how to get in touch with you. Leave home at home and work at work. It's a great way to balance both. Have you ever been with others and you are conversing, only to look at someone in the group who is looking at their phone? How does that make you feel?

One of the issues I have seen in my coaching practice is loss of communication, and I feel a large part of that comes from electronics. Some people's idea of communication is texting and emails. Also, contemplate the detriment that comes from misunderstanding in texting and email. How it is written is not always how it is intended. Take your shot—silence!!!

I've had several restaurants and I used to "hit the ground running." Well...that catches up to you rather quickly and can cause health issues. **SLOW DOWN—CALM DOWN— WIND DOWN!** It is your power shot. It's all part of silence. All good things come from a calm state. Nothing good comes from stress, worry, or doubt. I continually discuss the importance of breathing, calming mechanisms, and winding down after a day at work. Nothing good comes from being in a hurried or chaotic state. The idea is to learn tools to assist you with increasing productivity, personally and professionally.

One tool for calming down is to **TAKE A BREATH!** Being able to focus on your breathing is a shot that will assist you with unwinding and letting go of the negative emotions.

Here is an example of a breathing technique:

- Close your eyes and take a very deep breath in through your nose
- Hold it as long as you can and then release it very slowly through your mouth
- Repeat this technique 3 times

This breathing technique will definitely calm you down. If it doesn't you are not doing it properly. Expelling the air through your mouth is the calming mechanism, but if you don't take enough in you won't have enough to let out.

I have so many clients who either say they don't know how to unwind after a stressful day or that their spouse can't unwind. The best time to unwind after work is on the ride home. Don't continue to have phone conversations after you leave work. Find something relaxing like listening to music or your favorite podcast. Taking a breath to unwind is a shot, but why not make it a double? Call your spouse to say, "I love you"—or just talk. The double shot is creating that positive connection to your spouse (connecting the dots). It will also alleviate the anticipation of what mood you will be in.

COMMUNICATION

You'll notice from the previous chapters that I frequently discuss the importance of communication. One area that some people struggle with is how their boss doesn't understand family issues. **TELL YOUR STORY!** Take the shot with effective communication. Communicate to your boss what your family obligations are so he/she is aware why you are taking a vacation day or why you need to leave work early. I've had many people tell me that they make up their time and their boss fails to recognize it. I always ask, "Did you tell them?" Maybe they are unaware. Communicate.

When my son was born, he had a life-threatening illness, which basically included hospitalization throughout kindergarten and first grade. I would get my daughter up in the morning and get her ready for school. Then I would go to the hospital to see my son. After leaving the hospital I would head straight to work and then return to the hospital on my lunch break. At the end of the workday, I would go back to the hospital and visit before going home. Upon arriving at home, I would help my daughter with schoolwork, cook dinner, clean up, get her bathed, and have a babysitter come to stay with her after she went to bed. I would go back to the hospital and stay until my son went to bed. In the morning, I would do the same routine.

When I accepted a new position, I failed to communicate to my boss what my personal obligations were. One day he was angry because I left work to go to the hospital, but it was truly my fault. I needed to make him aware of the situation with my son and I did not. You need to communicate personal responsibilities so your career will not be affected.

Setting boundaries allows you to say what you are willing to do and what you are not willing to do. Therefore, **JUST SAY NO!** Saying no helps you become a better friend and partner. It removes any guilt you may have.

Saying "no" clearly defines that you recognize that a particular action will cause you stress and you are not willing to partake in it. I don't feel you should say no to things you've committed to without validity, but you will certainly understand who your true friends are. True friends will understand if you change your mind or just say "no" without a specific reason. It will prove to them that you trust them and there is a sense of loyalty. Saying no is part of setting boundaries, but be careful how you communicate it. Always do it respectfully and honestly.

Learning how to say no is part of every aspect of your life, personally and professionally. Everyone and everything is affected by communication.

So, why not...**INVITE YOURSELF TO DINNER!** Make the call to your spouse and let them know you are looking forward to a great family dinner. When you get home, remember to silence your phone and SHOW UP! Family dinners that involve no cell phones, a calm environment, and engagement in conversation that concerns everyone's day is like hitting the jackpot!! You get to discover what is going on in everyone's life, and it's an opportunity for you to talk about your own goals. You can work through obstacles by brainstorming together to help someone who needs it, and you can plan family activities. Most importantly, you can show love and positivity.

ACCOUNTABILITY

So, you're probably wondering how you stay on track with all of these wonderful shots toward positive change.

STAND UP AND DELIVER! Take a shot and choose an accountability measure or partner. We all need some type of accountability to keep us focused and on track. It is so easy to be excited in the beginning, but we quickly fall off track. If you choose someone to be your accountability partner, choose them wisely. Make sure it is someone who doesn't push you so hard that you want to quit or feel like a failure.

Accountability, for me, is deadlines. I am an "A" type individual who can accomplish anything I set my mind to, but I tend to procrastinate. Therefore, my accountability measure is how I talk to myself. I am someone who sets goals and I include my accountability in my plan. Most successful people feel that procrastination is a negative, and it generally is. For me, it is not. I procrastinate until I am sure of what I need to do and why. I feel as though if I jump in to meet the deadline without full comprehension of the details, then I have created an NPA (non-productive action), which is a time waster. I love this quote:

> *"At the end of the day we are accountable to ourselves.*
> *Our success is a result of what we do."*
> —Catherine Pulsifier

Personal obligations can interfere with our job performance. It is very beneficial if you keep track of your productivity.

"ABSORB WHAT IS USEFUL...DISCARD WHAT IS USELESS...AND ADD WHAT IS SPECIFICALLY YOUR OWN!"

Consider that quote from Bruce Lee. Take it as your shot. It will help you with being selective about what useful things you need to allow in. Get rid of things that serve no purpose, and add the things that are all your own. This quote can assist you with understanding your Productive Actions (PA) vs. Non-Productive Actions (NPA)...otherwise, known as time wasters. If you learn to journal your day, you will discover your PAs and NPAs. This will allow you to eliminate all of the time wasters that are keeping you from reaching your goals. You will then be able to focus on your productivity. I think we all have those time wasters, but we may not be aware of what they are. That is why journaling is so beneficial. Non-productive actions can be toxic.

An additional method to holding yourself accountable is to **MASTERMIND FOR SUCCESS!** Forming a mastermind team is a wonderful shot you can take for staying on track and finding solutions. I'm sure you've heard the phrase "Two heads are better than one."

A mastermind group is five to six people who are likeminded. Choosing those who have reached similar success levels ensures continuity when seeking sound business advice. The group will generally inspire you toward motivation and determination. Choose people who are passionate about life and career.

I've been in multiple groups throughout my life. They've proven to be very beneficial. Mastermind groups create a win-win situation for all who participate by developing new friendships and business opportunities. The interaction of the participants creates energy and provides commitment and excitement.

Below are the benefits:

MASTERMINDING

- Challenges each other to create and implement goals, then holds you accountable.
- Allows you to brainstorm ideas and provides support backed with total honesty, respect, and compassion.
- Promotes growth and expansion in your business and personal life.
- Creates increased energy.
- Enhances interpersonal relations.
- Fosters an extension of your intelligence.
- Provides a reference point of expectations.
- Allows participants to support each other.

Each person's participation is key because you rely on their feedback, brainstorm new possibilities, and set up accountability structures that keep you focused and on track. You will improve your personal and professional life because everyone offers support and resources.

You can meet weekly, bi-weekly, or monthly. It's up to the group. However, try to keep your meetings limited to one hour and divide the time between the group. Everyone works together to help each other solve problems and keep motivation strong.

GOALS

Once you begin to work through obstacles and learn accountability measures, **START A GOAL—IT'S YOUR ACE IN THE HOLE!** What a perfect time to take your shot to start a goal. Why are goals so important?

The most important aspect in goal setting is to keep your mind on what you want and off of what you don't want. Example: If you are trying to eliminate debt, do not focus on bills. Focus on abundance. Striving for financial stability is a great goal. You can't do good without money. Begin to focus on finance with a positive mindset.

Having a goal offers the following benefits:

GOALS

- It serves as a map to make sure it is something you really desire.
- It will create an awareness of your strengths and weaknesses and guides your behavior. You can't contradict what you are able to afford; therefore, your goal must be aligned with your budget.
- A goal will provide you with challenges. This is part of your action plan.
- Goals require you to get organized. Write it out and then pull in your visualization techniques.

- A goal will help to eliminate procrastination, improve performance, and intensify motivation and persistence. These go hand-in-hand. You will need an accountability partner. This will increase your motivation, and you will then make it part of your routine.

- Having a goal increases your self-esteem. Once you have a clear direction, it will affect how you see yourself. You will begin to recognize success from within.

- You'll develop an attitude of gratitude.

- It will decrease negativity and increase positivity. They go together. Giving yourself positive instructions helps make it a reality.

Align your goal with all areas of your life. Ask yourself these questions:

1. How will you balance your career with family obligations?

2. How will it affect your spiritual and financial life? Money tends to be a problematic area for many people. Understanding and implementing faith will help you reach your goal without fear.

3. Will it impact you physically? It is imperative to instill good health habits.

4. If your educational background is not in alignment with your goal, what resources will you need?

5. Does your present career serve you, or do you need to make a change?
6. Are you able to grow in your present state?

Your goal begins with your ideas and imagination. Once you have the idea, you need to utilize your imagination and place it on the screen of your mind with exact detail. Details are what assist you with attaining successful results. For example, vision boards are very powerful once you have a goal. What is a vision board? It is a board you create with pictures that are in exact detail of your goals. You should look at it daily and say your positive affirmations aloud when you look at it.

The reason it is important to say your goal aloud is because "vibration" assists you in attraction. We are energy, and if you keep yourself in a positive vibration, you will attract positivity. If you remain in a negative vibration, you will attract negativity.

Goals will assist you with calmness because it serves as a map to provide you with direction. There are still many shots you can take to make your spouse and family feel as though they are part of your goals.

With goal setting, I suggest you **PUT YOURSELF ON YOUR "TO DO" LIST!**

Take a shot—schedule yourself. You are the most important aspect of your personal and professional life and we tend to get caught up with making "To Do" lists, so that we don't forget to take care of other people's needs. Well...take a shot and add yourself to the list!!

Being able to put yourself on your "To Do" list means that you need to eliminate things that will interfere with your priority of taking care of YOU!!

AVOID TOXINS! This is where you take a shot to set boundaries and discard those useless items. Setting boundaries is huge because it allows you to take pressure off and focus more on you. Don't do anything that causes you anxiety or resentment. It will provide you with extra time and energy for your own personal development. You should always put your needs before the needs of others because you know what best serves you, your job, and your family. Plus, you will gain the respect of others.

Taking a shot, in addition to setting boundaries and saying "no," is to... **LOVE FROM A DISTANCE!** This particular shot is to begin assisting you with a plan to put someone at a distance. If you feel you are being controlled in any way, that is your indicator to distance yourself. This is an opportunity to begin learning how to say "no." Did you ever have someone who tries to manipulate the conversation? If so, that is negative energy. If you try the effective communication method and they are still trying to silence you and control your thoughts, words, or actions, then love them from a distance. All of those things compromise your joy. It is difficult to walk away from friendships even if they are toxic. Of course, every relationship is worth trying to save, so find a respectful way to communicate what you feel is wrong. If it turns into a negative situation, you may have to re-evaluate the friendship.

PAMPER YOURSELF

Begin to take a shot: **TAKE A COFFEE BREAK!** In coaching it is difficult for me to get people to get out of a hurried state. We tend to dive right into the day or the situation. Taking the shot to take a coffee break is so much more than that. It is about finding extra time and indulging in the moment. Most people will tell me that they don't have time to take a morning coffee break. Well...I will tell you that you can't afford not to. There are many shots you can take to assist you in being able to do that.

First of all, get as many things done in the evening as you can. This will free up time in the morning. You can make your morning go so much smoother if you can get up before anyone else. This will provide time to check emails, meditate, journal, and most importantly...take time to quiet your mind with a great cup of coffee (or anything you enjoy). When you get yourself in a calm state of mind you will be far more productive.

It is not selfish to think of yourself. It is imperative that you are happy and content so that you remain in control. All of the shots in this chapter will assist you in getting yourself to the proper place. Once you have taken a few shots you will be in a great place to take a shot to **DRESS UP—SHOW UP—LIVE IT UP!** One area of concern is the stay-at-home mom (or dad) complaints. Many of them feel badly that their husbands (or wives) are able to "be away" all day from the daily stressors and then get to go to an after-hour event or business meeting. Sure, they are still working; however, they get to experience "winding down."

The shot is to include your spouse by taking him/her with you. Call and get them excited about getting dressed up and showing up...then make it a great evening. Live it up!

Being a stay-at-home mom or dad is one of the hardest jobs. You never get a break from the home environment and daily responsibilities. Take the time to express your gratitude for them. They don't get the reward of a paycheck written out to them or some of the business perks.

It doesn't matter if you are the stay-at-home mom/dad or the person who goes to work. Everyone contributes. It is your job to always find the shot to create simplicity of appreciation.

Now that you aren't just making a living, you're making a life. You'll see the benefit to take a shot for personal development.

CHAPTER 4

INVEST IN YOURSELF—BECOME A BETTER PERSON

*"The only person you are destined to become
is the person you decide to be."*
—Ralph Waldo Emerson

*"Personal development is the belief that you are worth the
effort, time, and energy needed to develop yourself."*
—Denis Waitley

Personal development is the most important aspect of your inner being. Your every action and habit will affect every area of your life. It is key to learn tools that will help you be positive. Positivity will help you both physically and psychologically. All of the chapters in this book go hand-in-hand, but ultimately, everything begins and ends with you. You can change anything in your life and overcome all obstacles if you modify your behavioral patterns. Begin the change you need to make a difference in the world.

AWARENESS

YOU DO YOU! Take that amazing shot!!! With everything you've learned or recognized...it truly is all about you. This is a new phrase that I hear a lot of people using. It makes perfect sense to me. Taking the first shot is about you investing in yourself and building your character. So, if you don't take care of you...what happens? You become lost and everything falls apart.

How do you take care of yourself?

We previously discussed slowing down so you can recognize things that need to change. Well, once you slow down physically, you need to slow down in your mind. Calmness of mind is important for change and productivity. As I previously stated, I ran wide open for many years. I thought I was a great multi-tasker...greatest mass producer of productivity. I was wrong. Once I learned to slow down, I found that I was far more productive. **BUILD YOUR FOUNDATION!** This is the most powerful shot in personal development. It is your inner strength. In my years of coaching and owning multiple businesses, I found you cannot just hand someone a plan. You need to get to know them—first and foremost—and then create incremental steps toward change. That is why taking the first shot is so important. Building your foundation is equivalent to making a "3-pointer."

When someone hires me, they realize something needs to change...they want to be different. Therefore, they need to build a new foundation. Just as a house needs a foundation so the house will stand strong, we need an internal foundation of strength that will support our strategic plan of action. I continually mention slowing or calming down, so you can think more clearly. A foundation consists of strength, durability, and the insurance of sustainability for future improvement. Well...your internal foundation is the same. It consists of three components with the same definition.

REPEAT YOUR MANTRA! Meditation is your strength. The mantra is a positive word to focus on. Reflect back to the previous chapters when I discussed mental muscles. You get your mind strong and calm. As I stated, mental exercise is comparable to physical exercise. When we learn to meditate, the calmness provides the strength to support our new habit in a positive way. There is no right or wrong way to do it. Many people get very frustrated because they are unsure of the procedure. I would suggest that you begin with guided meditation because you won't have the ability to immediately get your mind clear. Guided meditation consists of someone helping you maintain mind control by presenting a positive message, and the remainder of the time is spa music. The ultimate goal is to have calmness without thinking of anything. Deepak Chopra offers wonderful meditation tapes that help guide you and keep your mind on positivity. Our minds tend to wander, so the positive messages assist you with focus until your mind is strong enough.

Some people do not like to hear someone talking and they prefer some sort of calm music. Remember, choose what works for you. The ultimate goal is to learn to meditate in total silence.

SPEAK THE TRUTH! The second part of your internal foundation is positive affirmations, which is durability. Continual repetition of positive statements. It provides resilience to the meditation. Positive affirmations are extremely effective and will assist with turning negatives to positive. You need to say your affirmations in the positive tense. Examples:

"I can..."

"I will..."

"I'm grateful now that..."

I always say that you can't trick your mind, but you start by tricking it. That is controversial, but it is kind of like the saying, "Fake it till you make it." You align your positive affirmations with your goals and you continually work on action toward those goals. Your positive affirmations strengthen your mind to believe that you can achieve those goals and they become permanently fixed in your mind.

JOURNAL YOUR JOURNEY! The third part of your internal foundation is <u>journaling.</u> This is your insurance of sustainability for future improvement. Your physical foundation needs to support years of improvement and sustainability. Well...journaling is how you track your progress while building the strong part of your foundation. Most people hate to journal, but I tell them that you don't have to write a book. Just a few words to show how you are progressing. For example, journal your negatives so you can see how long you stayed stuck in it. Once you make progress, you learn how you are able to get rid of the negative situation quicker. You may have stayed stuck in a situation for weeks and once you begin journaling, you will learn how to get down to days...hours...minutes.

Now that you have a solid foundation, it is time to **RISE AND GRIND!** Daymond John (with Daniel Paisner) wrote a book called *Rise and Grind*. It is to teach how to outperform, outwork, and outhustle your way to a more successful and rewarding life. So...push yourself to the limit.

Once I figured out what I needed to change, I began to see glimpses of success. However, I knew I needed more. I wrote my first book but knew nothing about the publishing industry. I started to read the importance of having someone write a foreword. I had no idea who could help me or how I could even get to know someone famous. I loved the teachings from Bob Proctor, but never met him. I began to wonder how I could get him to endorse my book, so research became my new focus. It was a Friday and I had an idea. I called one of his representatives to potentially sign up for one of his programs. When the man began the conversation, I asked him if I could speak to Mr. Proctor. He chuckled a bit and said, "I'm sorry, but he is unavailable." I continued to tell him I wanted to speak with him and he said, "Yes, everyone would like to speak with him. Even if I wanted to call him, he is in California and it is only 6:00 a.m. there." I said, "Call and wake him up." Again...he laughed. We went back and forth a bit and finally he said, "Hold on."

After little time had passed, he came back on the line and said, "I'm going to connect you to Mr. Proctor." I heard this tired voice say, "This is Bob Proctor. I don't know who you are, but this better be good." I was so excited that I accomplished this, but was a bit frightened as well. Long story short...we talked quite a while and then I asked him for his endorsement. He told me he would read the book and if he liked it, he would endorse it. I ended up going to one of his events and he gave me an audio endorsement for my Revolutionize series. That was my Rise and Grind. He changed my life. I followed his every word and suggestions and it worked. My whole life turned around due to his teachings. Those teachings have worked hand-in-hand with my education and life experiences to assist me in becoming a very successful life coach.

Once you have the internal foundation built, you can make many positive changes. Your foundation is the 3-pointer that will put you far ahead of the game. It is the strength you need to push your limits so that you attain success. There are many shots you can take after the hard work of the foundation is complete.

For example: **FOLLOW YOUR HEART, BUT TAKE YOUR BRAIN!** Sometimes our heart gets in the way. However, if you have learned how to slow down, you will be able to follow your intuition. It is your gut reaction that coincides with your other mental muscles in your brain. Your intuition is your sixth sense. We all have intuition, but some of us need some assistance to develop it. Test your progress on small things. For example, when you are in a store and you need to make a decision on a purchase, choose the one that comes to mind first.

We tend to analyze our decisions. Become aware every time you have to make a decision. You'll begin to notice how many times you begin to analyze choices. Start to test your intuition. Once you have gained strength in your mind, your mental muscles work simultaneously with your heart. What a winning combination!

Once you've learned how to develop your intuition, you will be able to **PLANT YOUR GARDEN!** Take a shot and pay attention to what you are placing on the screen of your mind. Planting your garden begins with planting seeds. So...plant positive seeds in your mind. This is the visualization process. When I previously discussed goals, I talked about creating a vision board. This process is very important when you are planning your goals. When you begin planning your goal, be sure to pay attention to what you are placing on the screen of your mind.

I explained how the visionary process is important for your goals. Therefore, if you pay attention to any negativity that you place in your mind, you will begin to discover your saboteurs. Your saboteurs are what causes bad habits. When you begin to counter the negatives with positive seeds, be sure to use your positive affirmations. The visionary process is a combination of the picture you place in your mind and the positive affirmations you verbalize. Be cautious and don't forget to weed. If you do not remove the weeds from your garden, they will ruin the beauty.

COMMUNICATION

The information so far might begin to become overwhelming so there are many shots you can take to begin working on making small, positive changes. Sometimes we need to take a basic shot and **GARGLE!** Get the bad taste out of your mouth!! So many parts of our life are filled with negativity and a small part is how we look at things. Make an attempt to think about the areas that cause you discomfort or anger. Rid yourself of that taste and welcome the sweet side of people and situations. You can do that quite easily with an **ATTITUDE OF GRATITUDE**. Being grateful creates an internal feeling of positivity and appreciation for all the things in our lives, big and small. You should be saying five things you are grateful for every day, and they should be different each day. You will appreciate everything positive in your life, and it will even help change how you communicate.

So, how do we do that?

I'll give you a few shots to take that will assist you with feeling good about yourself. **DON'T BE A STRANGER!** Fire away...you won't miss. Say something nice to someone you don't know and remember that every person loves to hear something nice. Pay attention to the demeanor of the person you compliment. I do it all the time and it truly touches my heart to notice that I made someone smile. We get caught up with so many daily distractions that sometimes we don't notice others. I mentioned earlier that sometimes electronics plays a role in us not recognizing our own loved ones, so, after you slow down, think about the strangers you meet that you don't even notice.

Sometimes a stranger may have a bad story. It is not your job to figure out everyone's struggles, but you can still **HELP A HOMELESS PERSON!** I wish I could help them all, but that is unrealistic, so if we all stand together, we can help one person at a time. Unfortunately, there are people who abuse the concept. There are many people who beg for money so they can buy drugs or alcohol, but there are still ways to make a difference. For example, put bags or purses together that contain items to help. You can place a gift card to a store where they can purchase items they may need. Or, you can put many items in your bag, such as blankets, pillows, etc. One thing that is a great idea is a booklet with resources in it. Maybe they need a phone number to an organization that can provide them assistance with turning their life around. There are many ways to help.

Taking a shot to help others makes you feel great inside. There are so many ways of making others feel good, which should assist you with motivation. Take a few minutes and think about all the insignificant things people complain about. For example: restaurants. I've been an owner in the restaurant industry, and it amazes me what people complain about. Not all people go to a restaurant and complain. There are so many complimentary and wonderful tipping people out there, but at the same time, there are a lot of people who are extremely hurtful to wait staff. **COMPLAIN ABOUT WHAT'S WRONG!** WHAT??? How can that be taking a shot toward becoming positive? Well...that's my point. There are times that it is beneficial to complain as long as you do it calmly and effectively. A negative connotation can be positive. For example, a good restaurant owner welcomes feedback about a negative situation so they can correct it and work towards perfection. However, it's about presentation. There are positive ways to convey a negative situation.

Sometimes you are very dissatisfied with your meal or your server. Take a shot and look at it differently. It shouldn't always be about the food, but the experience.

And sometimes, we have a bad experience in every aspect. A few examples of why someone is dissatisfied in a restaurant: food is cold; it's taking too long; you received the wrong meal; or maybe, you just don't like it. As I previously gave you tips on effective communication, the same applies in these situations. There is no reason you can't find something positive. Always begin with a positive. Any of the examples I provided could be the fault of the chef or the wait staff, so focus on something they are doing right and begin with that.

You can then begin to convey the complaint in a calm manner. Remember, they are not going to intentionally provide you with a bad experience.

The other side of the coin is to take a shot and **TIP YOUR HAT!** Tipping shows a sense of appreciation for a fine dining experience. Do the extra-ordinary. I tend to tip the cook, and it is a very satisfying gesture to see the astonishment. Most people don't do it. I'm not saying to tip everyone all the time, but if you can afford it and your experience was great...why not? You feel better and they feel better. I understand that many people feel as though they are not financially able to tip, but you should be aware that tipping is part of dining out and it is a critical part of a server's income.

Helping and giving to others is a wonderful suggestion, and that is why I feel charitable contributions are great. Remember taking the shot of the three S's in the children's section? Teaching our kids to share at a young age will help them share as adults.

CREATIVITY

There are hundreds of shots you can take to make a difference in others and yourself. Don't forget about the **You Do You** shot. There are those times that something small can have a big impact. For example: **PAINT A ROOM!** Take a shot to change. Change isn't always about our personal appearance or personality. Taking a shot to make an environmental change can bring satisfaction. Painting, redecorating, or buying something new can help us improve our mood. If you don't like it, you can always repaint.

I have many clients who say materialistic changes don't help and that is perfectly okay. This book is intended to give shots you can take that will make a positive change for you. If only one idea brings you joy, it is the beginning for change.

Why not take an additional shot to **TAKE UP A NEW HOBBY?** We all have talents and abilities within ourselves. You can discover new things you are good at by making the attempt to go a different direction. Taking up a new hobby and getting out of a rut can also assist you with conquering fears.

How?

TAKE A LEAP OF FAITH! That was the shot I took to help me overcome my fear of heights. Fears consist of many things, such as spiders and snakes, but it can also be fear of failure, success, death, etc. My leap of faith was to fly in an open cockpit WWII bi-plane, ride a zip line, and jump off a tall platform. My heart was racing, and I was in a full-blown panic attack, but I did it. Once you face your fear, you begin to realize that you CAN do it, which is the motivator you need. Don't get me wrong...just because you face it doesn't mean you'll like it. I hated the experience of jumping off a platform and wouldn't do it again, but it gave me personal satisfaction to know that I was willing to make change. Now, on the flip side I loved flying in the open cockpit airplane. With everything I continually do to rid myself of fear, you begin by looking at the positive side and coaching your mind in the process. It is quite rewarding when you do something extraordinary and like it.

There are those times we need to be away from things and people. **ROAD TRIP!** Taking a trip can bring a lot of joy to your life. It can be a family trip, a get-away for you and your spouse, or it can be a trip for you and your friends. There are many people who say they can't afford to take a trip. As I mention throughout the book, not everything takes money. You can pack a basket, grab a blanket, and have a great family outing. If you want to do something with your friends and can't afford a trip, find common interests and be creative.

The point of these shots is trying to assist you to **RE-CALCULATE!** That's a shot to take for sure. It is a great idea to try a different direction if your current route isn't taking you where you need to go. It may be taking a shot in the direction of material things, habits, or maybe just looking for personal change. You will discover why you need to recalculate as you continue with goal setting. Once you figure out why, start planning your new route.

When positive change occurs, you will begin doing new things in a different way. Recalculating will become automatic. Once you begin breaking bad habits, your environment will become positive.

Creating a new, positive environment will change your personality. **DON'T BE JOE COOL! LOSE THE HYPERSENSITIVITY!** This loss (hypersensitivity) will be a winning shot! We tend to take many things to heart. Take a few moments to analyze your sensitivity. Being overly sensitive can lead to arguments, hurt feelings, or negative talk. Your emotional sensitivity can affect your relationship, friendships, working environment, children, etc. Take a step back when you feel you are becoming hypersensitive to a situation and analyze your reaction. Begin to ask yourself questions about the situation.

- Am I overreacting?
- Is it worth it to be emotionally negative about this situation?
- Were the intentions of the person purposely mean or am I taking it wrong?

There are many ways to calm down before you react in a negative way that may cause more issues. You can utilize many shots that I have talked about to help you become aware of your reactions. There are also shots you can take to assist you with turning your negative behavior to positive.

POSITIVITY

Now...**BREAK THE NEGATIVE CHAIN!** The negative chain is an additional result of hypersensitivity. Once you react negatively, it will cause the domino effect. We tend to complain about the situation and others tend to feed off it. If you keep your sensitivity in check, you won't be a part of the chain. Dealing with things on our own will eliminate tendencies to create drama.

Remember, in all the areas we are discussing in this book, we are the ones who self-sabotage. So many situations can be eliminated if you utilize the tools to take the first shot. It is so much easier to be negative than positive. Negative is the dominant emotion. Negative and positive cannot occupy the mind at the same time, so guess who wins? You need to work harder to override negative with positive. I always use the example of weather. I continually hear people say, "There's 50% chance of rain." NO...there is also 50% chance of sunshine.

Why don't people say the positive?

So many people will tell me that they are positive, but once you begin to listen to them, you will begin to see how the negatives slide in.

Taking the first shot will definitely begin the process of turning negatives to positives and assist with goal setting. Remember, you can always **CROSS THE BRIDGE!** When you cross the bridge, you get to the other side. We create the negativity and generally tend to blame it on other people or circumstances, but if you think about it, YOU and only you, have the ability to accept or reject everything. Therefore, for all the negativity you accept...that is what you get. You can now take a shot to cross the bridge and get to the other side...positivity!

Forgiveness is a very big one. Many people won't forgive and what they don't realize is that forgiveness is about you and not the other person. Some situations are very serious, and you may realize that you shouldn't be around certain people. Well, for those circumstances, forgiveness helps you to move on. You don't have to hang out with them again or place yourself in a negative situation. It will just allow you to be at peace.

If you are unable to forgive, it's like the ship that can't sail away because it is tied to the dock. You want to be able to untie the rope and sail out to see the beauty and peacefulness of the water.

The first step to forgiveness is **RELEASE THE BEAST!** Recognize the situation for what it is, and then in order to move on you need to release. I'm sure most people have heard of "writing a letter." It is actually very therapeutic. You write a letter to the person who hurt you, but you don't send it. You don't focus on grammar or punctuation...just write. Say anything you want to release your hurt or anger. Then, place it somewhere that no one else will find it. Take it out in a week, read it, and put it back. Do that again until your anger is gone. After you don't feel hurt or anger... burn it. Burning it is letting go. It is totally symbolic, but it impacts your mind to be rid of it and realize the person is not worth your energy.

I've personally encountered some very serious situations that had a major negative impact on me. By recognizing the situation and then being able to release, I no longer allow it to affect me negatively. It feels so wonderful and it brings a sense of peace. Forgiveness is a powerful tool that sets you free. Free from allowing negative thoughts.

I've taught my children to forgive people and situations that most wouldn't. My thought process is that everyone makes mistakes. Some people change and some don't, but if you don't forgive and give an additional chance, you will never know what could've been.

In this personal development chapter, it's about taking shots to begin changing negative behavioral patterns. Think about habits and where they come from. There are times I will repeat myself from chapter to chapter and that is because I want you to retain some very important facts. We talked about the power of your mind and that negative and positive can't occupy the mind at the same time. Also, I explained the conscious and subconscious mind, so you fully comprehend where your behavior originated. Being that your conscious mind is your reasoning mind, you have the ability to accept or reject any thought at the conscious level. Once you've accepted it to be true it moves into the subconscious mind, and that produces your results...your habits.

Changing behavioral habits will assist you with taking a shot to **GET OUT OF YOUR RUT!** Getting out of your rut consists of getting into a new routine, mindfully and physically, and exploring other options for pleasure. We tend to do what we know and are used to. Getting out of your rut is to get out of your comfort zone. Familiarity brings more of the same. Try to think of something you normally wouldn't do and then...do the opposite. What does that look like for you? Try it...you might like it.

Now that you have taken the shots to invest in yourself and become a better person...take a shot to create a perfect health plan.

CHAPTER 5

OPEN YOUR HEART TO PERFECT HEALTH

*"It is health that is real wealth and
not pieces of gold and silver."*
—Gandhi

*"Strength does not come from the physical capacity.
It comes from an indomitable will."*
—Gandhi

Creating a healthy lifestyle will not only increase longevity, it will help you make better decisions that will improve your life personally and professionally. Adopting healthy choices will impact you psychologically for positive growth. It's not solely about the food we eat or the exercises we perform. It is also about the things we put in our minds. Negativity and stress can cause physical and psychological issues. Eat healthy, exercise, and be positive—protect the only life you are given!

PERSEVERANCE

DON'T TAKE THE ELEVATOR...USE THE STAIRS! Take a shot to a heart-healthy start. Two years ago, I woke up with a debilitating illness. The doctors couldn't figure out what was wrong. I am a very healthy person with a lot of energy, so it's been difficult. However, one thing that has helped me on my road to recovery is my mind. It is extremely difficult to push ourselves out of our comfort zone and to have the internal power of will to surpass pain.

Why?

Because it is easier to ride in an elevator than to endure the pain of the stairs. The thing most people don't realize is that the endurance of the pain brings mental satisfaction. Plus, it assists us with physical strength. For example: I was unable to take the stairs unless someone held on to me. I pushed myself mentally and physically to surpass the help. It wasn't easy and I won't bore you with the lengthy process, but after two years, I CAN take the stairs by myself. Does it cause pain? Yes, but I keep pushing.

So, whether you begin to take the stairs to lose weight or surpass the pain, it's a shot that will motivate you to continue on your journey toward a healthy life. **BE A FRAUD!** Take a shot and go to the gym. Not only are many people unmotivated to create an exercise plan, they are also fearful they can't do what others can. Be a fraud by faking it. You are not being dishonest. No one knows your capabilities... even you, so, tell yourself that you CAN and WILL (positive affirmations) do it!!

Everyone had to start somewhere. When you look at the people who are truly conditioned with going to the gym, you must realize that they started at the beginning. If you still have doubts about taking a shot, then begin by taking a step and calling the gym for details. Or, better yet, go take a tour. Do not focus on the seasoned people—focus on the beginners. Making healthy choices isn't just about exercise. It is about the foods we eat. Even if you don't need to lose weight, you may need to be in tune with the foods you put in your body.

POST A STICKY NOTE! This is a shot you can take to place your weight on the screen of your mind. Write your ideal weight on a sticky note and place it on the scale so when you step on it, that's the number that will stick in your mind. There are so many clients who put their program in place and then check their weight each morning. If their weight stays the same or if they gain, they are discouraged and many of them discontinue their plan. No!

By placing the sticky note, you don't focus on the number, but how you feel. If your clothes feel good on you, it becomes a motivator. If you didn't place the sticky note and your clothes felt good, but the scale was slightly tipped, you would not be motivated. There are many factors that trigger weight gain, such as water.

GAIN WEIGHT—HYDRATE! Believe it or not, some people won't drink water because it makes them feel full or bloated. They actually think it makes them gain weight. What they don't realize is that you truly need water to assist you with a healthy lifestyle. There you have it. Take that shot and drink the water...WATER WEIGHT IS GREAT!

WHY HYDRATE?

- Weight loss
- Increased focus and memory
- Healthier skin
- Enhanced mood
- Healthier bowels
- Joint lubrication
- Healthier muscles

Maintaining a healthy weight and incorporating exercise is beneficial for longevity. There are too many things that can go wrong with our health, so make the choice to do everything you can for self-improvement. People think of health as just diet and exercise, but it's about so much more. As I previously stated, learning internal calmness and positivity is a very healthy choice.

COUNT YOUR CHIPS (NOT YOUR POKER CHIPS... YOUR POTATO CHIPS)! I know that sounds silly, but you would be amazed as to how it impacts your mind. It is a re-programming as to how you look at food. Here is an example: Tell yourself that you are allowed eleven potato chips per week. Once you do that you are giving yourself permission to have fattening foods, but you will be able to control how many you eat and how often. You see, I help people with weight loss and they tend to relapse because of their perception. When you tell them "no chips," it's a negative. However, starting them out with allowing is a positive. They will begin to plant that seed (remember...

negative is the dominant so you need to override it with the positive). After a while, most people end up not eating the chips at all. It is a process to retrain your mind.

An additional shot relative to counting that will help you break a bad habit is to **GO UP IN SMOKE!** This is good for smoking cessation. I have a complete weight loss and smoking cessation program. Counting your cigarettes is the mental aspect of it. I begin by having my clients lay out the number of cigarettes they smoke each day and begin by removing one each day or every other day. The visual image of the cigarettes works by changing your mindset. Visualization is the aid that works simultaneously with your willpower.

Reprogramming your mind is difficult, especially with losing weight. You incorporate positive affirmations, calmness, and journaling (part of your foundation that we discussed earlier). That is where you gain strength. You can't begin by just eliminating and putting negative rules in place. If you make it gradual, it is easier (breaking down to manageable pieces). Counting chips, removing cigarettes, or placing a sticky note on the scale will not eliminate the habit. It is an aid that works with the program. I gave the examples to show that visual aids have an impact on changing your mindset.

AWARENESS

FLIP A COIN! Take a shot to make a decision—CALL IT! To accomplish the items I talk about in this chapter you must first make a decision. We all have choices—good or bad. The bad lifestyle choices will cause health issues and decrease longevity. Again, it's not just about eating and exercise. Negative personality traits can cause health issues as well. Alcohol, drugs, lack of sleep, anxiety, stress, fears, bad habits, worry, and doubt all play a negative role. The shots throughout this book are intended to assist you with positive, healthy choices.

BENEFITS OF HEALTHY CHOICES

- Weight loss
- Increased energy
- Mood enhancement
- Diabetes, heart, blood pressure, and disease management
- Improved memory
- Better sleep habits
- Better choices for the next generation
- Reduced stress
- Increased productivity

There are many people who are not aware of the benefits of healthy choices. Once you begin to recognize the impact of everything you put in your body, the positive choices will become easier.

ACT LIKE A MONKEY! The old saying "Monkey see, monkey do" is a process without an understanding as to why it works. Whether it's imitation in a good sense, bad sense, or instinct, it is ultimately copying the behavior of someone or something. So, why not make healthy choices to improve upcoming generations. Think back in history of the negative or positive things that continually impacted those close to you. I continually discuss people's limiting beliefs and how they impact our lives going forward. If we accept a negative belief to be true, it molds us into creating habits, fears, etc. If we plant positive beliefs and habits, the next generation will have a positive impact.

This is especially true in children. When they are born, they have nothing to compare things to, so if you tell them the sky is purple, they would believe it. In my coaching program I discuss the developmental periods of a child's life and how it is impacted. From birth to age seven is the IMPRINT PERIOD, where everything is absorbed from the environment. You are your child's environment so be careful what you do and say. That is why I am discussing "Monkey see, monkey do."

From age seven to fourteen is the MODELING PERIOD, where they begin to model behavior from outside sources, such as friends, family of friends, models, movie stars, etc. This is where many problems can occur because they are easily influenced by other people and things. I have many parents who ask me how they raised two children exactly the same and they turned out different. That is due to the modeling period. The children break away from immediate family and start hanging out with friends with different interests. Each child chooses different types of friends and that is where it starts to branch out.

From fourteen to twenty-one is the SOCIALIZATION PERIOD, where they become individualized. They combine things from the other periods of their lives and then form their own beliefs. Therefore, it is imperative that you understand that your behavior, your lifestyle choices, and the influences of other people and circumstances begin to form the upcoming generation.

Understanding what influences assist with how your child develops will help you make better choices. I coach a lot of children, and it continually amazes me how the actions of the parents truly influence what the kids think about. And remember...thoughts become things, so let's work together so that the children have good, positive, and healthy thoughts.

Now that you've learned how to open your heart to perfect health, discover how you can deal with an elderly loved one when they begin to lose their healthy lifestyle.

CHAPTER 6

REMEMBER WHEN? AS OUR LOVED ONES AGE

"The wiser mind mourns less for what age takes away than what it leaves behind."
—William Wordsworth

"Age should not have its face lifted, but it should rather teach the world to admire wrinkles as the etchings of experience and the firm line of character."
—Ralph B. Perry

Watching our elderly loved ones causes many changes and challenges. The intention of this chapter is to help you and your family take a look at the tough situation you may be experiencing. Look through the eyes of your loved one and try to imagine how they feel. No one wants to be a burden, and when physical and psychological challenges occur, they get very scared. It is unfamiliar territory. Close your eyes, look into your heart, and please be patient. Someday, you may experience what they are going through. Treat them as you hope you will be treated.

AWARENESS

TURN UP THE HEARING AID! This is a powerful shot to take because it will influence many aspects to the person who is aging and the family members who must provide daily care. Getting old can be very scary because of the health changes. Caring for those we love as they age can also be frightening, due to all the demands from the health issues. Many of those issues can be less complicated if we just turn up the hearing aid so we can LISTEN to what they are saying...or trying to say.

Think of the frustration as a middle-aged individual. As the years roll by we tend to feel some daily aches and pains, but take a moment to close your eyes and imagine the frustration if you were to have decreased hearing, difficulty with your eyesight, or limited mobility. You would begin to feel inadequate. Now, think about the ones you love becoming frustrated with you. You wouldn't understand because when you were on your "A" game, there was normal conversation, love, and laughter. And not that you don't love the elderly, but there are many people I know who get frustrated. Trust me...the elderly sense that frustration. It can cause them to become depressed.

Hearing loss is very common as we age. It stems from disease, heredity, noise we've experienced throughout our lives, and basically aging. Some signs that your loved one may need to consider a hearing aid:

- Difficulty hearing telephone conversations
- Can't understand people who are soft-spoken (especially children)
- Turning up the volume on the TV so loud that it annoys others
- Continually asking people to repeat what they say

The onset of hearing loss generally comes on gradually, so we get frustrated when it gets worse. Try to make it easier for the person by paying attention to their facial expressions and gestures. It will also make a difference if you face them while you both are conversing. You can also look for a place to talk that is quiet. Background noise makes it worse. However, the number one point is to be patient and kind. You may have to ask them to repeat what they've said, or you may have to repeat what you say.

There are many setbacks for the elderly that directly affect us, so be patient and **PASS GAS!** Let it all out and let it be! Elderly people tend to pass gas and not realize it or lose control of their bowels. People don't like to discuss it, but it needs to be addressed because we are all affected by the physical and mental changes. As we age, there are many health factors for losing control.

Some examples are:

- Alzheimer's Disease
- Diarrhea
- Muscle damage
- Cancer
- Nerve damage
- Stress

You can discuss options with your doctor. However, here are a few suggestions:

- Medicine
- Exercise
- Surgery
- Diet
- Hygiene
- Toilet time (let them spend extra time for toileting)

The main suggestion, once again, is to educate yourself so you have a complete understanding as to what is going on and then BE PATIENT! Someday YOU will BE THE PATIENT!

COMMUNICATION

I have many clients who come to me for assistance with coping mechanisms for Alzheimer's disease. It is an awful experience for the patient, so it is vital that we all learn how to cope. Take the shot to **INTRODUCE YOURSELF!** As the disease progresses, there are times you will experience unfamiliarity. It is so sad for the caretaker, because they don't understand how a parent or loved one doesn't recognize them. They are generally in and out of familiarity and every situation is different. There are many stages of the disease, but I highly recommend that you educate yourself, so you know what to expect.

Alzheimer's is a progressive disease that destroys memory and other mental functions, such as thinking and reasoning. It usually comes in stages and begins with general memory loss that disrupts a person's ability to function independently. It may cause difficulty for completing familiar tasks or problem solving and slowly progresses to confusion with time, people, and places. They tend to misplace things, experience poor judgement, and can even become withdrawn.

In order for you to effectively communicate with your loved one you will need to learn coping skills. These tools will help you deal with the person who has the disease.

COPING SKILLS

- Keep it simple. Everything should be presented one thing at a time.
- Keep a daily routine so they can get used to habits.
- Focus on their feelings, not their words.
- Use humor so they do not feel like there is something wrong with them.
- Work with your doctor to provide a diet and exercise program.
- Utilize things that will distract them in a positive manner, such as music, singing, or dancing.
- Ask them to help you do something, so they still feel needed.
- Whatever you do...DON'T argue with them, and when they tell you something that isn't realistic, just agree.
- The number one tip I have is to reassure your love and support. DO NOT get angry or frustrated with them. It's not about you. If you are frustrated, leave the room. Learn breathing exercises to calm down.

Many dementia and Alzheimer's patients tell stories that aren't true. For example, I recently visited someone who has Alzheimer's and they began to tell me about all the pink birds they were seeing outside. They asked me if I thought they were pretty and I said, "Yes. They are very pretty." It is okay to agree with them. It won't hurt anything. If I would've told the person there weren't any pink birds, they would have realized that something was wrong. Continually correcting them makes them feel sad and inadequate.

In the very early stages, **REACQUAINT YOURSELF WITH FAMILY MEMBERS!** Act as if you are just beginning a journey with a group of people. Learn patience in the early stages and prepare yourself early on. Families experience ups and downs throughout life; however, when a parent experiences medical issues, or mental disease (dementia or Alzheimer's), family members can experience opposition with one another. Remember the first few chapters when I discussed the developmental periods of a child's life? Well, that is why family members are so different from one another. There are cases where family members agree on everything and remain close; however, there are those instances where they become torn apart.

Some of that happens when parents get to those difficult stages. There are families where one person lives closer to the parent(s) and their responsibilities are greater. I repeatedly discussed the importance of effective communication, and that it is key in every aspect of our lives. This is no different. Try to understand that every person has a different perspective and emotional level. It doesn't make anyone right or wrong. The key is allowing each person to have their own opinion and then being mature enough to find balance. Balance is the secondary key to every aspect in life.

BALANCE

Take the next shot to **BALANCE YOUR BUDGET!** Many family members allow money to interfere with the most important issue—a parent's well-being. In the beginning I discussed the detriment of entitlement in children, but I've seen many clients actually experience the same as adults. They begin to argue about what is in the will and who is contributing to their care.

It's okay if one family member spends more on their loved one. Not all family members have the same income; therefore, each person should financially contribute without expectation of reimbursement. Remember—there is a solution to every problem. When a family has multiple members, you should never think of things as equal. It is okay if one does more or contributes more than the other. It is more beneficial for the parent if each family member stays focused on the issues in front of them.

Even though it is okay if one family member does more, one person should never be left carrying all the weight. Take a shot to **JUGGLE THE WEIGHT!** This will provide the balance you need to make sound decisions. Effective communication will allow you to have family meetings to discuss strengths and weaknesses of each person. One person may have the ability to contribute more financially, while someone else might have additional time for care. Find what works for each and meet in the middle.

Balancing the weight will assist you with letting go of expectations of one another. Recognize the needs of all siblings and their families. There are so many scenarios, so being flexible will allow for smoother discussions.

If you find yourself in a position where you can't come to a unanimous agreement for the well-being of the parent, then take a shot to **INTERVENE, BY ALL MEANS!** Pull in an outside resource to assist you with finding a solution. It may be that you are all too close to the situation and that emotions are high. I've personally experienced families being torn apart because of disagreements on end-of-life decisions, and that is wrong. Each person should respectfully have their own opinion, and if you can't find resolution, then have an intervention. Choose someone who has never been involved with your family to assist in the decision-making process.

Make sure you listen to one another before you react. Everyone's opinion is equally important. It is a tough situation for everyone so prioritize the most pressing concerns. In many cases it is beneficial to hire an additional caregiver. If you decide to hire outside assistance, remember to be respectful of that person. They also need balance to care for your loved one and their families. The demands of caregiving can become overwhelming. Having an outside intervention will also assist the family by eliminating burdens.

In many cases, families aren't emotionally strong enough to keep the situation positive. I've provided many shots you can take to assist you with the balance you will need. If your family falls apart, your love wasn't strong enough. Opinions should never cause destruction. Try to come together as a team! **GO THE EXTRA MILE!** Take a shot to spend additional time with your loved one so you keep good memories on the forefront of your mind. Try to coordinate a schedule between family members so time is covered. Don't look at the time that is required as a negative or a burden. It is your loved one, and the most important factor is providing love and support. The patient is the one who is enduring a tough transition, so please take a shot to make it comforting for everyone.

Do not make it burdensome...enjoy your time with them and feel good about helping out. **DO THE UNEXPECTED!** Take a shot by showing up and doing the unexpected chore and then hang around and reminisce about the old times. Being with an elderly parent is like being with your child. Don't look at it like it is something you have to do.

Nutrition and sleep affect the process of aging so discuss options with your doctor to implement a plan. Studies are constantly showing the benefits of a healthy diet. Sleep patterns change with aging so try to ensure that your loved one gets the required amount of rest. Mental stimulation is also very important so when you visit, play mind-strengthening games, look at family photos, listen to their stories, but most of all...

ENJOY THEM AND CHERISH EVERY MOMENT!!!!

You've learned how to take shots to assist with the transition of your loved one to a place of unfamiliarity. Discover how to take a shot to overcome the obstacles within friendship.

CHAPTER 7

THE INTERPERSONAL BOND OF FRIENDSHIP

"You can make more friends in two months by becoming interested in other people than you can in two years by trying to get other people interested in you."
—Dale Carnegie

"Many people will walk in and out of your life, but only true friends will leave footprints in your heart."
—Eleanor Roosevelt

"A real friend is one who walks in when the rest of the world walks out."
—Walter Winchell

Friendship is very important. We spend a lot of time with our friends and they are people whom we share our secrets with. Throughout life all relationships have good times and bad, but any relationship is worth saving. In order to learn tools to save friendships, you must also be able to identify if the relationship is healthy and positive.

Take a look at yourself, then take a look at your friends—be the change you're looking for in someone else.

AWARENESS

CLEAN OUT THE COBWEBS! Take the shot to make good decisions within your friendships. We all have those few friends whom we've had since childhood. The ones who grew with us like family. Being loyal, trustworthy, and understanding makes those friendships so wonderful. Although there are times, going through life, that we experience difficult friendships, it's okay to clean out the cobwebs and re-evaluate wants and needs of those relationships.

I have many clients who asked to be coached through the difficulties of some friendships. As I previously stated in the last chapter concerning family members, the same holds true for some friendships. It doesn't need to be measured equally. Each friend may be in a different position; however, you need to analyze the requirements of the friendship. Values are extremely important so make sure you share common ideals. There should never be requirements. If they are friends who continually take advantage and expect so much from the relationship, it may be time to take a shot to **TAKE THE EXIT!** If you are following the same route and getting the same results, you may need to temporarily find a new direction. All friendships are worth the attempt to save. You need to evaluate your relationship.

Ask yourself questions about the friendship:

- Is your friend jealous of you?
- Is your friend demanding?
- Are they negative?
- Do you feel anxious around them?
- Do they get angry with you easily?
- Do they have high expectations?
- Are they understanding when you break a commitment?
- Does everything have to be equal between you?
- Do they share the same values?

A friendship should be easy, not difficult. Once you self-reflect on the answers to the questions, you may recognize that your friendship is toxic. We never want to hurt others, but if you feel the person is not good for you then you may have to consider ending the relationship.

You can begin by spending less time together. Begin by not reaching out anymore. Let them message you and don't respond immediately. Simply become less accommodating. You also need to set boundaries. If you make yourself unavailable and they begin to challenge you, then you may have to end the friendship entirely. If you decide to end it, please do it by effectively communicating.

You can tell them that you've shared many enjoyable moments, but you've changed. Explaining it by showing that you have taken a different path will alleviate sadness. It takes courage to walk away from a friendship so please think it through very carefully. Try to reflect back in this book about effective communication. Do not begin any sentence with "You..." Begin with "I..." statements. It shows ownership and they'll begin to notice that you have changed.

In some instances, the friend becomes extremely dominating. If you experience pressure or bullying, just take a break. Let them know that you need a little time to think about the friendship.

You don't have to follow the pack. It is very healthy to go your own way. I always say that if I see 100 people walking one direction and just one person goes in a different one, I would follow the single person.

COMMUNICATION

There are times we get so emotionally involved and fear hurting someone that we put up with things that we shouldn't. This book is intended to help you take shots to work toward positivity and growth. Friendships shouldn't be work...they should be easy. You should definitely trust your friend to the point that you don't worry about every little word you say or action you take. A true friend is someone who understands there is no underlying intention for hurt.

DON'T TAKE THE BAIT! Do NOT respond to the attack! If you encounter anything in the friendship that represents an attack, then you need to analyze what you have. I continually discuss effective communication, so if you find yourself in a position of constant defense, then you are probably in a toxic friendship.

I'll give you an example: I feel as though friends need to understand that circumstances change. A true friendship should be one of honesty, so if you make plans and you change your mind for no apparent reason, it should be okay. Now, if you make extensive trip plans where expense or vacation at work plays a role, that's different. But, if you made small plans and just don't feel like going, everyone should understand. Don't make it complicated.

All relationships take work, but close ones should be minimal. There are times you need to take a step back and analyze your inner self. Take a shot and **LOOK IN THE MIRROR!** Ask yourself questions to discover what role you play in the disagreement or frustration with a situation. If you played a negative role...own it!! Owning mistakes is taking responsibility, and it is a basic fundamental principle of life and success. Owning it will assist you with making positive behavioral changes. Remember the chapter that discusses recognizing and releasing? Owning it is part of that.

Once we recognize and own our part, we stop blaming others. Regardless if it is your fault or the fault of your friend, you should always be able to come to a resolution. If you can't, then it was never a true friendship. **SWEEP OFF YOUR OWN DOORSTEP!** Eliminating negativity, drama, and blame is easier if you are able to take a shot to sweep off your own doorstep. It's about looking at mistakes you made in the past. It is one step beyond looking in the mirror. When you begin to make positive changes, don't judge others for things you are guilty of in the past.

Everyone makes mistakes. Instead of judging that person for something they are doing that has a negative influence, begin to encourage them to work toward positive changes. Let them know that you made the same mistake, BUT you've corrected the behavior. Teach them how you overcame the negative and replaced it with positive. Once we have made positive changes, we tend to forget things we have done wrong throughout our lives. Hopefully, we have all matured and wouldn't make the same mistakes. If someone you care about makes a mistake, make the attempt to understand and help them correct it. No one is perfect, and if you keep an open mind you will make it a positive experience.

WON'T YOU BE MY NEIGHBOR? Take a shot to be like Fred Rogers, the host and creator of *Mister Rogers' Neighborhood*. BE THE FAVORITE NEIGHBOR!! Don't judge someone who doesn't fit into the lifestyle you've made for yourself. When the program aired, he was a portrait of a man in a zip-up cardigan sweater who took us beyond the land of make-believe. BUT, he was a creative genius who inspired children and adults with limitless imagination and compassion. That's who and what we need to be.

Be that person who goes above and beyond. Become an inspiration to others. Be authentic. Being true to yourself will assist you with compassion. Caring about others helps build character. Life is full of challenges so don't create negative ones. Challenge people to do their best and live up to their full potential. It is leading by example. Everyone wants to feel good about themselves, so inspire them. Share your own stories of success and failure.

In my coaching business I encounter the little kids, the teenagers, the young adults, the stay-at-home moms, the blue-/white-collar workers, the entrepreneurs, and everyone who just wants to make a positive change. Who are you and who do you want to be? I believe in the saying **"WHAT YOU SEE IS WHAT YOU GET!"** Pull in all of the shots within this book so you can have what it takes to be a better person...an inspiration! Make a difference in you, us and everything else! We all experience the temporary motivation to be the person to make the difference. Life slows us down. Get up and don't give up!

You've taken the shots to help keep your friendship alive, so begin to enhance gratitude, strength and love.

CHAPTER 8

THE FINAL CHAPTER—LOVE, GRATITUDE, STRENGTH. . .LIFE!

"You've gotta dance like there's nobody watching.
Love like you'll never be hurt.
Sing like there's nobody listening.
And live like it's heaven on earth."
—William W. Purkey

"Gratitude is the fairest blossom that springs from the soul."
—Henry Ward Beecher

"Whenever you find yourself doubting how far you can go,
just remember how far you have come.
Remember everything you have faced,
all the battles you have won,
and all the fears you have overcome."
—Unknown

"Nothing can dim the light that shines from within."
—Maya Angelou

This entire book has been about my education, life experiences, mentors, great friends, and most importantly...positive changes. There are four stories that have truly made a difference in my life and have touched my heart and my life.

MAKE SENSE OF YOUR SENSES!

LOVE

The first is about a video I came across called **"The Seven Wonders of the World."**

A group of students were asked to list what they thought were the seven wonders of the world.

Most voted were:

- Egypt's Great Pyramid
- Taj Mahal
- Grand Canyon
- Niagara Falls
- Empire State Building
- St. Peter's Basilica
- Great Wall of China

While gathering the votes, the teacher noted that one quiet student hadn't turned in the paper yet. She asked her if she was having trouble. The girl replied, "Yes, a little. I couldn't quite make up my mind because there were so many." The teacher said, "Well, tell us what you have and maybe we can help."

> The girl hesitated, then said she thought the seven wonders of the world are:
>
> - To touch
> - To taste
> - To see
> - To hear
>
> She hesitated again and added:
>
> - To feel
> - To laugh
> - To love

The room was so full of silence you could have heard a pin drop. Those things we overlook as simple and ordinary are truly wondrous. This story is a gentle reminder that the most precious things in life cannot be bought; they must be experienced.

Think about that story and how important it is to teach the precious people we brought into this world (without them asking) good values—values that can make a difference in the next generation.

"It is never too late to be what you might have been."
—George Eliot

I hope the shots you fire will help you bring emotion, positivity, love, and laughter to your life and the lives of others. This is a story about my son when he turned sixteen. It is a story of gratitude that makes me so proud.

GAIN AN ATTITUDE OF GRATITUDE!

To give...is an essential part of being grateful. Since my children were born, I've continually instilled the gift of giving and gratitude. When they were young, I would encourage them, at Christmas, to give a gift that would have been from them. As they became older, we would participate in the Salvation Army's Angel Tree Program, and eventually we started our own. I would continually give to someone in need throughout the year and tried to teach them that it's not just about giving gifts. You need to help someone in need.

While owning one of my businesses, I had the opportunity to experience an exceptional employee who would go out of their way for the business and for me. My children were sixteen and nineteen at the time, and they both recognized the sacrifices this employee made. This individual had two jobs, did not have a vehicle, and would ride a bicycle to work...never being late.

My daughter was about to pass down her vehicle to my son. Being sixteen years old, I am sure he was excited to receive this vehicle; however, he decided to give the vehicle to this employee. It bothered him that someone could work two jobs and still have to ride a bicycle to work. He said he would work additional hours to save enough money to purchase a different vehicle...and he did. He worked enough to purchase a car and a computer for college.

BURN YOUR BOATS!

STRENGTH

The next story is about **"Burning the Boats."**

Think about the ancient Greek warriors who were both feared and respected by their enemies for their reputation of unsurpassed bravery and commitment to victory. Once the warriors arrived on the enemy's shores, the commanders ordered them to "burn the boats." With no boats to retreat to, the army had to be successful to survive. As the soldiers watched the boats burn, they realized there was no turning back—no surrendering. The same stands true in your own life and where you have arrived. That is why I love this story; you have no excuses for failure. You MUST "win" or perish. I have personally used this process to attain my own personal victories. It is a huge leap of faith! Think of all the missed opportunities within your own life because you didn't burn the boats.

Remove those obstacles and excuses;
Storm the shore with a successful attitude;
Let your fear and regret burn with the boat;
Leave it at the bottom of the water.

You WILL be victorious! Imagine the psychological impact on the soldiers when they realized there was no turning back. It removed any notion of retreat from their hearts and thoughts of surrender from their minds. In your own scenario, you will not battle on the shore, but you will battle in your mind.

"Every failure brings with the seed of equivalent success."
—Napoleon Hill

"Success is not final, Failure is not fatal;
It is the courage to continue that counts."
—Winston Churchill

LIVE BETWEEN THE NUMBERS!

LIFE

The fourth story is my legacy. A story that changed my life!

The Dash

by Linda Ellis

I read of a man who stood to speak at the funeral of a friend. He referred to the dates on the tombstone from the beginning—to the end.

He noted that first came the date of his birth and spoke of the following date with tears, but he said what mattered most of all was the dash between those years.

For that dash represents all the time they spent alive on earth and now only those who loved them know what that little line is worth.

For it matters not, how much we own, the cars...the house...the cash. What matters is how we live and love and how we spend our dash.

So, think about this long and hard; are there things you'd like to change? For you never know how much time is left that still can be rearranged.

To be less quick to anger and show appreciation more and love the people in our lives like we've never loved before.

If we treat each other with respect and more often wear a smile...remembering that this special dash might only last a little while.

So, when your eulogy is being read, with your life's actions to rehash, would you be proud of the things they say about how you lived your dash?

> *"Sometimes you will never know the value of*
> *a moment, until it becomes a memory."*
> —Dr. Seuss

I hope the shots you can fire from reading this book will help you with losing fear, making positive change, and having the motivation to win the game of life.

> *"Be the change that you wish to see in the world."*
> —Gandhi

GIVE...GIVE A LITTLE MORE...THEN, BE GRATEFUL!!!

REFERENCES

Bob Proctor, business consultant, motivational speaker, personal development coach, bestselling author

Daymond John with Daniel Paisner, authors of *Rise and Grind*

Dr. Robert Anthony, www.thesecrettodeliberatecreation.com

Dr. Steve G. Jones, hypnotherapist, NLP trainer, author, executive and personal development trainer, www.stevegjones.com

Jack Canfield, author, motivational speaker

Steve Harrison, co-founder of National Publicity Summit

ABOUT THE AUTHOR

 PEGGY CARUSO is a certified executive and personal development coach, author and 8-time entrepreneur. She is also the founder and host of "The Revolutionize Podcast." Her education also includes business and certification as a relaxation therapist and NLP (Neuro Linguistics Programming) master practitioner.

Peggy has written 4 books in the "Revolutionize" series and has been trademarked through the United States Patent and Trademark Office.

They include:

Take the First Shot
Revolutionize Your Corporate Life
Revolutionize Your Child's Life
Revolutionize Your Life

Peggy has been interviewed by NBC, CBS, Success Magazine, Reader's Digest, Franchise Handbook, Advancing Women, and has been a guest on radio and podcast shows across the U.S.

She is an expert problem solver, both personally and professionally, and is committed to assist people with reaching their goals. Her mission is to use part of the book sales to start a non-profit academy for children.

Peggy has two children (Nikki and Josh) and two stepchildren (Lindsey and Kira). She is the proud grandmother of one grandson (Jordan).

CPSIA information can be obtained
at www.ICGtesting.com
Printed in the USA
JSHW021208190121
11046JS00001B/37

9 781631 951398